BENEFACTORS

Michael Frayn's new play is about helping others. About helping them professionally; helping them privately; helping them readily; helping them reluctantly. It is also about an even more difficult activity: being helped. Being helped professionally and privately, and being ready or reluctant to accept. The action of the play takes place over fifteen years — time enough for both the helpers and the helped to be changed by their relationship; even for the helpers to become the helped, and the helped to become — still more in need of help than they were before.

Benefactors is published to coincide with its premiere in London in spring 1984.

The photograph of Michael Fr...........
Gerson.

Michael Frayn

BENEFACTORS

A play in two acts

METHUEN · LONDON

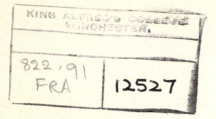
A Methuen Paperback

First published in Great Britain in 1984
as a Methuen Paperback original
by Methuen London Ltd, 11 New Fetter Lane, London EC4P 4EE
Copyright © 1984 by Michael Frayn
Set in IBM 10pt Journal by 🅰 Tek-Art, Croydon, Surrey
Printed and bound in Great Britain
by Whitstable Litho, Whitstable, Kent

ISBN 0 413 54160 6

CAUTION
All rights in this play are strictly reserved and application
for performance etc., should be made *by professionals* to
Fraser & Dunlop (Scripts) Ltd., 91 Regent Street, London W1;
and *by amateurs* to Samuel French Ltd., 52 Fitzroy Street,
London W1P 6JR. No performance may be given unless a licence
has been obtained.

Characters

DAVID
JANE
COLIN
SHEILA

ACT ONE

Three entrances — left, right, and centre.
Left: a large wooden kitchen table and half-a-dozen chairs, with other comfortably worn kitchen furnishings. Right: a single bleak upright chair.

DAVID *and* JANE.

DAVID. Basuto Road. I love the name!

JANE. Basuto Road. How I hate those sour grey words!

DAVID. Basuto Road, SE15. And at once you know when it was built and what it looks like. You can practically smell the grey lace curtains in those little bay windows. Don't you think?

JANE. You look back in life and there's a great chain of cloud-shadows moving over the earth behind you. All the sharp bright landscape you've just travelled through has gone grey and graceless.

DAVID. Basuto Road. But when you think how fresh and hopeful that must have sounded once, back in 1890! There's the whole history of ideas in that one name.

JANE. There it is, on the box-files all along the shelf — Basuto Road, Basuto Road, Basuto Road. Grey-faced reproachful words, shuffling towards you out of the shadows. I look away — and there they are again, running downwards on the chest where he keeps his old drawings — Basuto Road, Basuto Road, Basuto Road.

DAVID. Also Bechuana Road and Matebele Road and Mashona Road and Barotse Road.

JANE. Then ten years, fifteen years away behind you the land's out in sunlight again. You can see everything small and shining in the distance — so clear you feel you could reach out and touch it.

DAVID. Plus Maud Road, Daisy Road, Frances Road, and Phoebe Road. I suppose they were the builder's daughters. Rather sad — it's all coming down. About fifteen acres. What do you think?

JANE. Basuto Road. It started in the sunlight. He was happy then. Yes! He was! He was happy! He came back in the middle of the day to tell me about the job, and he was like a child with a new bicycle. Ten years ago? No, twelve or more. But that day, at any rate — that's out in the sunlight again.

DAVID. It's probably an impossible site. It's jammed between a railway line and a main road. What do you think?

JANE. He couldn't sit still. He couldn't stop talking about it

DAVID. It's zoned at 150 to the acre. I bet it's more like 200. I'll need you to check that for me.

JANE. We were both still children. Middle-aged children.

DAVID. But that would mean housing for 3,000 people. It's probably not possible. What do you think? If it's possible the council wouldn't be asking me — they'd be doing it themselves. It would be a huge job — I'd have to double the size of the office. But that's where the work is, Jane, in local authority housing. That's where the real architecture's being done. So what do you think?

JANE. What *did* I think? I don't know. I can't remember. I expect I was against it. I expect I raised all kinds of sensible objections. That was the way we operated then. David was for things; I was against them. Government and Opposition. And we'd always settle the question democratically. One for, one against — motion carried.

DAVID. I'll go and have a quick look at the site. Ring Bill, oh, and Geoffrey Lewin. Tell them I've been called away. Emergency. Job falling down.

Exit DAVID *centre.*

JANE. And that was fair. Because when I voted against I was really voting for. In those days. Anything David was for I was for. I wasn't going to tell *him* that, of course. Why not? I can't remember. Not that I needed to tell him. He knew perfectly well. Anyway, I had to come out in favour of this project soon enough, because Colin was against it.

Enter COLIN *left.*

David was for it, so Colin was against it. Colin was against it, so I had to be for it. It was like the start of a game.

COLIN. I gather David's landed one of these great slum clearance jobs. Changing the face of London. So he's on his way to the Rolls-Royce and the knighthood.

JANE. Not that Colin cared much. Not then. He was mildly sardonic. But then he always was. He didn't think about it. We none of us thought about it.

COLIN. What do you think about it, Jane?

JANE. King opposite king. Queen on her colour.

COLIN. I said what do you think about it?

JANE. A twilight area.

COLIN. A twilight area?

JANE. Not a slum clearance scheme, Colin. Not a slum.

COLIN. A twilight area. It sounds very beautiful.

Enter SHEILA *and* DAVID *left.*

JANE. Isn't that right, David?

DAVID. What's that, my love?

JANE. Basuto Road — a twilight area.

DAVID. It's certainly not a slum, whatever a slum is. No worse than this neighbourhood, really. Or no worse than it used to be. A bit grey and exhausted, that's all. Little weary shops where they sell maroon cardigans and dusty sanitary fittings. Little places under the railway arches where they respray cars and stable rag-and-bone men's ponies. You get a few surprises, too. There was a brand-new red Mercedes parked in Bechuana Road yesterday.

COLIN. A rival architect.

DAVID. A richer one than me, obviously.

COLIN. Or some demolition contractor sizing the job up. Like the hangman taking a look through the peephole.

DAVID. It's got to be done, though, Colin.

COLIN. Oh, it's got to be done. Otherwise the areas where architects and demolition contractors live will start to look a little grey and exhausted again.

DAVID. I don't know why I put up with you, Colin. Everybody else takes me seriously.

COLIN. I take you seriously, David. You're building the new world we're all going to be living in.

DAVID. You sit at my table eating my food and drinking my wine . . . Where's your glass?

COLIN. Sheila takes you seriously, anyway. She thinks the future's right there inside your head, like a chick about to burst out of an egg.

DAVID. I might as well have my father round all the time.

COLIN. Though she might feel rather at home in a sunset area.

JANE. A twilight area.

COLIN. Wouldn't you, my love?

DAVID. And don't start on Sheila, for God's sake.

JANE. Anyway, Colin, it's got to be done. You know that in your heart. We've got to rebuild areas like that.

COLIN. You're going to be working on this one, are you, Jane? Down there with the clipboard? Knocking on doors, doing the market research?

JANE. I don't do market research.

COLIN. Good morning, madam. Would you like your house pulled down?

DAVID. They're going to get their houses pulled down whether they like it or not. And we don't need to ask them what they want instead because we know.

COLIN. Nice little semis with nice little gardens.

DAVID. The best popular housing so far devised.

COLIN. But you're not going to build them nice little semis with nice little gardens.

DAVID. I can't! I've got to show a net housing gain, not a colossal housing loss. What do you get with semis?

COLIN. Aesthetic typhoid, I expect.

DAVID. You get about thirty persons to the acre. I've got to house something more like 200. I'd have to cover the site with one solid fused mass of semi-detached house.

COLIN. Sheila thinks that sounds wonderful.

DAVID. Work it out for yourself. You were Senior Whatsit.

COLIN. Was I?

DAVID. I thought you were Senior Whatsit? At Eton, or wherever it was?

COLIN. Senior Classical Whatsit. Not Senior Town Planning Whatsit, like you.

DAVID. Difficult to rise above Senior Milk Monitor at my school.

COLIN. Wake up, Sheila. It's the barefoot boyhood again.

DAVID. Sheila's all right. Sheila's awake.

COLIN. She's not saying very much. Are you, my pet?

DAVID. She's talking more sense than some people.

COLIN. If only we could find out what Sheila wanted we'd know what everyone wanted.

JANE. Over dinner, this would be. The children out of the way. Occasional clicks and whimpers on the baby-alarm from their two across the street. Colin and Sheila — I don't know — they seemed to live round here. She'd leave the children here at some point in the day. That's what usually happened. Then when she came to collect them she'd sit down for a cup of coffee and sooner or later she'd be saying, 'This is awful — I haven't done anything about the children's tea.' And I'd say, 'That's all right — they can have something here.' And then next thing I knew it would be, 'This is terrible — I haven't done anything about getting a meal for Colin.' And I'd say,

'Give him a ring — we've got plenty.' And she'd say, 'This is awful — we seem to live round here.'

DAVID. They're not here *again*?

JANE. Your friends, not mine.

DAVID. Sheila's *your* friend.

JANE. Sheila's *not* my friend.

DAVID. They seem to live round here!

JANE. You were the one who told them that house was coming up.

DAVID. *That* house! Not *this* house!

JANE. Anyway, I thought we were supposed to be helping them?

DAVID. I've been helping people all day. I've been helping 200 people to the acre. I don't want to help people all evening.

COLIN. How's Basutoland?

DAVID. Don't *ask* me . . . Sheila . . . I don't want to talk about it. I've spent most of the day with the Regional Architect and the Regional Quantity Surveyor, and they say it may take a year just to establish the Yardstick with the Ministry. I can't get hold of the Borough Planning Officer, and the Borough Engineer has sent me on to the GLC Planning Department because the site's next to a trunk road, and they say I've got to consult the Ministry of Transport, and I know what they'll say, they'll say no, categorically no access. So that's all I know — there's no access to the site. I don't suppose it matters about access for residents, we can do without residents, we don't want to provide housing for anyone — God forbid! — they've only got 14,000 on the housing list — but I've got to provide access for refuse vehicles, because there's a union agreement about the maximum carry, and I've got to provide access for ten-ton fire appliances, and get the furthest door within range of a ninety-foot hose, and I've got to provide lifts deep enough to accommodate stretchers and coffins, and I still haven't seen the District Surveyor or the Superintending Architect of Metropolitan Buildings. I expect they've got a few more tricks up their sleeve for stamping out housing in London.

COLIN. All right, then, David — don't.

DAVID. Don't what?

COLIN. You said you didn't want to talk about it.

DAVID. I don't want to talk about it. I've been talking about it all day. Have you opened some wine? I'm not going to go high. But if I don't go high we won't qualify for the high-rise subsidy, and if I don't get the high-rise subsidy I won't meet the Yardstick, and if I don't meet the Yardstick we won't be rising at all, high or low. And for God's sake don't ask me what the Yardstick is . . . HCY 1. Housing Cost Yardstick 1 . . . And of course I'll fight. We'll reach compromises, I'll get waivers. But when I think of the struggle it's going to be! When I think of all the words, all the paper, all the anger, all the dust, all the mud . . . Because I'm not going to build towers. No one wants to live in a tower.

COLIN. I'd like to live in a tower.

JANE. Colin, why won't you ever be serious?

COLIN. I am serious. You build a really high tower, David, and I'll come and live at the top. Surrounded by silence. Silence and empty sky.

DAVID. Don't be silly, Colin.

JANE. The lifts would keep breaking down. You know what these places are like.

COLIN. Perfect.

DAVID. You'd never meet your neighbours. You wouldn't see a living soul from one week's end to the next.

COLIN. This isn't a block of flats you're describing, David. This is paradise.

JANE. No, we liked them. We really did. I wasn't just running a soup-kitchen. Well, we liked him. David liked him. But he did actually urge David to build tower blocks! Quite funny when you think what happened later. It was just part of the game, of course. David was against them, so Colin was for them. He wasn't serious. David pretended not to be serious, but in fact he was. That's why Colin could always get a rise out of him.

Colin one end of the table, grinning. David the other end, frowning. Me putting in a word here and a word there, trying to redress the balance. And Sheila sitting there like the Dormouse, not saying anything at all.

COLIN. Come on, my love. You've talked enough for one evening.

DAVID. More wine? More coffee? More something?

COLIN. Which of us has the harder task, do you suppose? You, getting rid of us; or us, getting away from you?

COLIN and DAVID go off centre.

JANE. I can't think now which year that would have been. Sixty-nine, I suppose, or seventy . . . Mind Jake's frog farm thing in the hall . . . !

Exit JANE centre.

SHEILA. Sixty-eight. That was the year. He started on Basuto Road in April, just after Lizzie's birthday. They were such good friends, it was lovely. You felt you could always pop across the road for a chat. I used to go flying over there at all hours. I'd just slip a coat round my shoulders and push their front door open, and — Hoo-hoo! And Jane would be rushing around, doing fifteen different things at once, and I'd sit there in the kitchen and watch her and I'd think, Oh, if only I could be like that! If only I'd got her energy! And the colours of everything in the kitchen were so warm and friendly. And David would come popping in for a moment on the way to one of his sites, and the children were lovely, and they'd all make you feel you belonged there.

Enter JANE left.

I cry sometimes now when I think about it.

JANE. Poor old Sheila.

Exit SHEILA right.

Always flying over with some new disaster. The washing-machine had overflowed — the lavatory was blocked — Matt or Lizzie was ill. Matt and Lizzie were always ill. You'd be working in the kitchen, say, and you'd suddenly become aware that there was this little voice somewhere in the house going 'Hoo-hoo . . . hoo-hoo . . . '

Enter DAVID *left.*

DAVID. I wish she wouldn't say hoo-hoo.

JANE. She's got to say something.

DAVID. We could lock the front door.

JANE. No, we couldn't.

DAVID. Some people lock their front doors.

JANE. Not us.

SHEILA (*off*). Hoo-hoo!

DAVID. If only she'd say, 'It's me', or, 'Anyone at home?'

Enter SHEILA *centre.*

SHEILA. Anyone at home?

JANE. Hello! Just in time for coffee!

SHEILA. Oh, Jane, I can't. Hello, David.

DAVID. You're looking lovely. Big kiss. See you later, I expect.

Exit DAVID *centre.*

SHEILA. I've got to get Matt to the hospital. He's got an appointment at eleven.

JANE. Eleven? I'd better run you there in the minibus.

SHEILA. Oh dear. This is awful. I must learn to drive.

JANE. We'll get David to teach you.

SHEILA. Colin would never buy a car, of course.

JANE. I hate them, too.

SHEILA. Then on Saturday I've got to get the children to my mother's.

JANE. Learn to drive, Sheila. Then you can borrow the minibus. Hold on, I'll get the keys.

Exit JANE *left.*

SHEILA. She must have thought I was awful, now I look back on it. I practically lived over there! The children would come looking for me, and they'd be hungry, and before I knew what was happening Jane would be making them baked beans and egg soldiers. Things they'd never eat at home they'd tuck into perfectly happily over there. Her children were older, of course. I suppose Matt and Lizzie being there was almost like having two more in the family.

Enter JANE *left.*

They'd all disappear upstairs to watch television together, and the next thing I knew there'd be a glass of wine on the table in front of me, and Jane would be urging me to ring Colin and stay for supper.

JANE. Well, you didn't get to the shops today, did you?

SHEILA (*into phone*). Hello, Colin? It's me.

Enter COLIN *right.*

COLIN. You're at Jane's.

SHEILA. I'm at Jane's.

COLIN. She's inviting us for supper.

SHEILA. She says why don't you come over and have some supper.

COLIN. You're in love with that woman.

SHEILA. She thought the children could have a bath here. They could sleep in the spare room.

COLIN. Did you hear what I said? I said you're in love with her.

SHEILA. He says that would be super.

Exit COLIN *right.*

JANE. She sometimes invited us back, of course.

Enter DAVID *left.*

DAVID. Oh no! No, no, no, no! I can't! I'm ill! I've got architect's elbow!

JANE. David, we have to make the effort once in a while.

DAVID. It'll be all cold and dark brown, and Colin'll be in a funny mood, and there'll be trouble with the potatoes.

JANE (*into phone*). Sheila, I'm terribly sorry. David's got a meeting on Wednesday evening.

SHEILA. Thursday? Or Friday? Or the following week some time?

JANE. Sheila, why don't I give you a ring when we've got clear of work and holidays and children and parents and things?

SHEILA. They came to us sometimes. A few times. But we went on walks together, we went on picnics. We always used to say, 'If we're going with the Kitzingers we know the weather will be fine!' And it was! It always was!

JANE. The children always complained about it, of course. 'Do we *have* to go with the Molyneuxs?' — 'Yes, we *do*!' '*Why* do we have to go with the Molyneuxs?' — 'Because we've got a car and they haven't.' — 'But they're so *boring*! And Matt and Lizzie smell.'

SHEILA. And once, when we were on our way back from somewhere, David took us to see Basuto Road. I can't remember what it looked like now. All I can remember is David making a great gesture with both arms, like a magician commanding up a vision. And me feeling terribly happy. I don't know why.

DAVID. Forget all these houses, Sheila. Forget all these little streets. What we've got is very roughly a triangle. Main road — Bechuana Road — railway. I'll tell you what I'm thinking of doing, Sheila. I'm thinking of a courtyard. Two sacrificial slab blocks . . .

Enter COLIN *right.*

COLIN. Two what?

DAVID. Sacrificial slabs. All right, Colin, all jokes in writing, please, on the back of a postcard. Two long slab blocks that sacrifice daylight on the outside to protect the rest of the scheme from the noise of the road and the railway. Six or seven stories high. Blind walls on the outside, and all the flats facing inwards into the morning and afternoon sun, on to the gardens and play areas, on to the life of the community.

SHEILA. It sounds a bit like your old college at university.

DAVID. Exactly, Sheila! Absolutely! I predict a first!

SHEILA. My God, have I said something right for once?

JANE. You've put your finger on the basic principle of all modern British architecture.

COLIN. The college wasn't seven stories high. We didn't have a railway running down one side of it.

DAVID. No, but she's got the general point. We felt like a community because the building had turned its back on the rest of the world.

JANE. What did the rest of the world feel like?

DAVID. *You* were in another college!

JANE. That's what I mean.

DAVID. Well, of course you were in another college! You were in a women's college! We were in a men's college! Don't be silly.

COLIN. How wonderful — a row! Don't stop!

DAVID. *I'm* not rowing.

JANE. *I'm* rowing.

COLIN. Sheila's withdrawn to a tactful distance.

SHEILA. No, no.

COLIN. Just a little chat about the old days, my pet. Look, she's feeling all excluded.

SHEILA. No, I'm not. I'm very interested.

DAVID. Come here, Sheila. My favourite pupil.

SHEILA. No, I was just thinking, it must be wonderful to change things. It must be magical to look at some new thing that wasn't there before and think, *I* did that!

DAVID. No, it's not, Sheila. It's heartbreaking. It's always just warped windows and condensation problems. It was going to be so new and amazing, and it never is, it's always just like everything else. I'll tell you what's wonderful, Sheila . . . I'm not talking to you two . . . I'll tell you what's really magical. A

bare building site. Something still quickens in me when I smell
that raw damp smell of green brickwork and wet cement.
When I feel the loose hardcore shift and grind under my shoes.
I love those huge holes in the ground when people are going to
go really high. Amazing emptiness, like the emptiness of a
conjuror's hat, because you know that marvels will come out
of it. I love looking at the site when it's like this, even — all
other houses, all clutter waiting to be cleared.

COLIN. Some elegant new concrete block in the East End blew
up last week.

DAVID. One flat blew up. There was a gas escape.

COLIN. The whole lot came down like a pack of cards.

DAVID. One side came down.

COLIN. Progressive collapse.

DAVID. Because it was system-built. The walls were holding up
the floors. I shall use a steel frame.

JANE. Come on. The children will be screaming with hunger.

COLIN. The words will outlast the building, even so.

DAVID. What words?

COLIN. Wonderful words. 'Progressive collapse.'

JANE, DAVID *and* COLIN *go off right.*

SHEILA. I knew what David meant, though. Something coming
— yes. Something new. Everywhere we went with them the
trees were alight with fresh green. And yes, we had rain
sometimes, of course we had rain — but a warm spring rain,
with something new and marvellous in the wind behind it.

Enter JANE *right.*

JANE. Then on Monday morning I'd be back down there. David
thought the council's figure for density was wrong. He was
afraid the mix was wrong, too — he was afraid there were
more small households than the council said. So I was up and
down those dull grey streets every day with my clipboard,
trying to find out how many one-bedroom flats he ought to
provide, how many two-bedroom . . . Basuto Road, Bechuana

Road, Matabele Road . . . Maud Road, Daisy Road,
Frances Road . . . There was never anyone in. Ring the bottom
bell. Wait. Silence . . . Ring another bell. Dog barking. Wait.
Next house. Ring. Silence . . . And then, as you turn to leave
some doorstep, you realise there are two faded, ancient eyes
inspecting you through the letter-box. You bend down and
speak to them. 'Good morning. I'm doing a survey of housing
requirements in the district.' The eyes gaze at you for a long
time. Then they speak. 'Oh, no, love. We're all Labour here.'
Bang. Try the next house. A black face looks round the door.
Black faces. A woman covered in children like an apple tree
with apples. 'Good morning. I'm doing a survey of housing
requirements in the district.' She laughs. Oh dear. Never
mind — plough on. 'I wonder if you could tell me how many
people there are in your household?' She puts her hand to her
mouth and laughs like a bird singing; she can't understand my
dialect. 'I see. Thank you.' In the next house some huge wild
animal flings itself against the other side of the door, audibly
slavering. Across the street I wait for minutes on end while
infirm and elderly footsteps struggle downstairs towards the
door. An ill grey face appears. 'Good morning. I'm doing a
survey of housing requirements in the district.' — 'It's my
mother, you see.' 'I beg your pardon?' — 'She's fallen out of
bed. I can't lift her.' And of course when I get up there it's not
just lifting she needs. So that's the morning gone.

SHEILA. I do admire you, Jane. I wish I could do something
really worthwhile like you.

JANE. Sorry, I've only just got back.

SHEILA. I do envy you, having the chance to get out of the house.

JANE. Do you want a quick cup of coffee before you fetch
Lizzie?

SHEILA. I'll do it.

JANE. Sit down!

SHEILA. But then you're good with people, aren't you.

JANE. People. I don't think I like people very much.

SHEILA. You're so good at helping people.

JANE. I ought to be. That's all I ever do. Help David. Help the children.

SHEILA. But that little boy down at Basuto Road. The one who'd been locked out by his mother.

JANE. Well, I couldn't just leave him standing there in the rain.

SHEILA. I wish I was like you, Jane.

JANE. Look, I'm not trying to help anyone down at Basuto Road. I'm just trying to count them. I keep my eyes shut as much as I can.

SHEILA. It's what I always wanted to be — someone who helped other people.

JANE. You are. You do. Don't be silly, Sheila.

SHEILA. I did, when I was nursing. I never seem to have the time to do anything these days. I think I *am* other people.

DAVID (*off*). Only me.

Enter DAVID *centre*.

Where are my Wellingtons? I'm supposed to be out at Finchley . . . Sheila . . .

SHEILA. It's like the wind rushing into the house.

DAVID. They should be in the car. They're *never* in the car . . . ! The wind, yes — that's what I'm going like today. Ten to three. Aren't you fetching Lizzie?

SHEILA. Oh my God! One day I'm going to forget her completely!

JANE. Coffee . . .

SHEILA. I'll have it when I come back . . .

Exit SHEILA *centre*.

JANE. Twenty to three. Do you want her coffee? You lent your boots to Daisy.

DAVID. That was a long speech.

JANE. What?

DAVID. Sheila just then. Oh, yes, Daisy. I think Sheila's a bit happier, isn't she? I think things are a bit better over the road.

JANE. Are they?

DAVID. Funny when he lived in that terrible flat, and we weren't supposed to know she existed. I'll never forget dropping him outside the door one day, and there was this unexplained pregnant belly trying to conceal itself behind the side of the porch.

JANE. I expect she'd locked herself out.

DAVID. I expect she had. I sometimes think he only married her because we happened to meet her.

JANE. We didn't *happen* to meet her. She came knocking on the door, saying Colin was in Durham and she was in labour.

DAVID. My first sight of *him* was saying grace in Hall. Very grave and unsmiling. Collar and tie, yellow flower in his buttonhole, scholar's gown; no shoes or socks. It was our first term. I can still remember the shock. The world wasn't really serious after all!

JANE. Imagine being married to him, though.

DAVID. Imagine being married to Sheila. Where did he pick her up?

JANE. Outside Lugano railway station.

DAVID. Thirty, and he was giving English lessons.

JANE. She'd had her rucksack stolen.

DAVID. Senior Classical Whatever-it-was, and he was giving English lessons in Lugano.

JANE. He's got a perfectly good job now.

Enter COLIN *right.*

There's no need to feel sorry for him.

DAVID. Working on a women's magazine?

JANE. Yes, but then he's got that encyclopaedia thing he does in his spare time. He's the editor of that.

DAVID. He's the entire staff, isn't he?

COLIN. Fornication . . . Fetishism . . . Frigidity . . .

Enter SHEILA *right.*

SHEILA. He'd spread it out over the living-room floor at night.

COLIN. Foreplay . . . Femininity . . . Fallopian tubes . . .

SHEILA. I'd just watch him sometimes. I couldn't have the television on.

COLIN. Father . . . Father-figure . . . Fun . . . I'll do Fun myself . . .

SHEILA. Did you say Femininity? I could do Femininity.

COLIN. What?

SHEILA. I mean, if you wanted me to.

COLIN. That's an idea. Jane could do Femininity.

DAVID. What's it called? Happy Families?

JANE. I don't think he chose the title.

DAVID. I mean, the bits you do are fine.

JANE. I think he takes it all quite seriously.

DAVID. But then you've got a degree in anthropology.

COLIN. How about the kids? Would they like to do a bit? Fathers? Foot fetishists?

DAVID. You're on to F already?

COLIN. F is for Funderwear. Sexy lingerie sales are booming. Leading psychiatrists now believe that even the happiest marriage can sometimes do with a little black silk ooh-la-la.

DAVID. All the same, a lot of people are going to find something like this genuinely helpful.

COLIN. Yes, you might benefit yourself. You might try looking under D for Domination.

DAVID. I'm always longing to be done good to.

COLIN. Symbols of male potency; towers, high-rise, getting the thing up — you'll find most of your professional life in there.

SHEILA. The trouble would be afterwards, when we got home.

You'd never know which way Colin was going to jump.
Sometimes we'd sit down and laugh about them.

COLIN. What should we do without them, my pet? What should
we talk about together, if we didn't have David and Jane?

SHEILA. When you said about putting towers into holes in the
ground! He didn't know where to look!

COLIN. He wasn't always so tamed and righteous. He was like a
wild hare — quick and timid and wide-eyed and cunning — and
he laughed and he smelt, and we were going off to Greece
together, and he came to my rooms one night and he said, I'm
not going to marry her — I'm not — I'm not!

SHEILA. Do you think they're sitting there talking about us?

COLIN. What would they do without us? We make them feel
good. It's our one contribution to the world.

DAVID. It's unpleasant for *her*. That's what I hate.

JANE. I think she rather enjoys it.

DAVID. Those little embarrassed laughs of hers.

JANE. I shouldn't worry about Sheila.

DAVID. I wish we could do something to help them.

JANE. We do! We just about keep that marriage together! What
do you think they're doing at the moment?

DAVID. You mean, talking about us? Talking about us talking
about them, probably.

JANE *and* DAVID *go off left.*

SHEILA. And sometimes he'd sit down, and I wouldn't know
whether he wanted to talk or not. I'd just know that whatever
I did it would be wrong.

COLIN. What?

SHEILA. Nothing. I was just thinking.

COLIN. Just thinking what?

SHEILA. Just thinking it was funny when he said about having
these, you know, by his Finchley site.

COLIN. These what by his Finchley site?

SHEILA. Strange erections.

COLIN. Don't try to make smutty remarks. It doesn't please me. Why do you think it would please me?

SHEILA. I'm sorry. I thought . . . I mean, you often . . .

COLIN. Don't try to ape me. Why do you think it would please me to see myself aped?

SHEILA. Please don't be like this, Colin.

COLIN. You think I'm so pleased with myself going out that I want to see myself coming back?

SHEILA. I just thought it was funny.

COLIN. Yes, I heard you laugh.

SHEILA. I didn't laugh.

COLIN. You're always laughing. You're the only one of us without a sense of humour, and you're the only one who laughs. But you don't know *when* to laugh, you see.

SHEILA. I didn't think I was laughing.

COLIN. You don't know *how* to laugh.

SHEILA. Please, Colin, please!

COLIN. You wouldn't start singing in public. You know you're tone-deaf. But you're deaf to all shades of relation and meaning. Go away. Go to bed. You disgust me.

Exit SHEILA *right.*

DAVID (*off*). Problems! Problems, problems!

Enter DAVID *centre.*

That's all my life consists of!

Enter JANE *left.*

I get to the office — there's a message from the site agent at Finchley. They've driven their ten-ton crane on to the children's play area. To their great surprise, their ten-ton crane is now in the drains underneath the children's play area. I get back to the office and there's this waiting.

SHEILA (*off*). Hoo-hoo!

DAVID. I can't build anywhere within six feet of that thing. So I've lost about a fifth of the site.

JANE. Couldn't they divert it?

SHEILA. Hoo-hoo!

Exit COLIN *right.*

DAVID. Oh, that bloody woman! Divert it? Yes, they could divert it, but that's going to cost about a thousand pounds a metre!

JANE. Couldn't you get them to cut back on parking-space?

Enter SHEILA *centre.*

DAVID. Hello, Sheila . . . Cut back on parking-space? What good would that do . . . ? Come in, come in.

SHEILA. Sorry.

JANE. If you didn't have to provide a hundred per cent off-street parking you'd have a bit more space and money to play with.

SHEILA. I thought David would be at the office.

DAVID. I'm just on my way down to see the Borough Architect about *this*!

JANE. The electricity people have got a 275,000-volt cable running across the Basuto Road site.

DAVID. So what — I have to go to eleven stories?

SHEILA. Oh dear. Poor David.

DAVID. You wouldn't believe what goes on under that site. Wires, pipes, sewers. It may not be buildable. Seriously. I may be building a piece of unbuildable land.

JANE. Back for lunch?

DAVID. I may not be back at all.

Exit DAVID *centre.*

SHEILA. Poor David.

JANE. It's his element. If you don't like problems don't take up architecture.

SHEILA. It must be awful for him, though.

JANE. Anyway, if you don't like problems don't take up living.

SHEILA. Poor David . . . Poor David . . .

JANE. Sheila, love, what's the matter?

SHEILA. Nothing.

JANE. Come on — you'll make me cry too. It's not the children?

SHEILA. No.

JANE. Colin?

SHEILA. No, no.

JANE. You haven't had a row?

SHEILA. No, no, no.

JANE. Sheila, we can't both stand here crying if I don't even know what we're crying about.

SHEILA. It's not anything. I don't know what it is. I'm sorry. I'm all right. I'm sorry, Jane. I'm fine. Everything's fine. It's just that . . .

JANE. Just what, love?

SHEILA. Just that . . .

JANE. I'll get us some coffee.

SHEILA. Jane, what should I do if he left me? How should I cope? I can't manage the children on my own! And what about the money? I can't help worrying about the money. What would I do? I can't go back to nursing — I have to collect Lizzie at three o'clock every afternoon. I just stand there in the kitchen after the children have gone off to school, and my thoughts go round and round — what should I do? — how should I manage? — and I can't get anything done, I don't know where to start, and I think, he can't come home again and find everything like this — I haven't even made the beds — and then I think, it's awful — I can't go running over the road again!

JANE. Sheila, take a deep breath.

SHEILA. I know you've got David's problems to worry about.

JANE. Sh.

SHEILA. You've got your own work to be getting on with.

JANE. Come on. Coffee. Still warm. Lots of sugar.

SHEILA. Oh, Jane . . . Oh, Jane . . . Whatever should I do without you?

JANE. Now, come on, love, don't start crying again. Just tell me. Has Colin said something about leaving you . . . ? There isn't anyone else, is there . . .? I think it's all inside your head, Sheila. You're shut away on your own all day so you start to imagine things.

SHEILA. I watch Colin in the evening sometimes. He looks round at the home we've made — that brown sideboard, those brown chairs — everything's brown! And I know what he's thinking.

JANE. Does he say what he's thinking?

SHEILA. No, he's very kind. He tries to be kind. But I know. And he's right! It *is* hopeless! *I'm* hopeless! I'm no use to him! He was lovely once. He was shining and dark and fearless and frightening. He didn't care if people hated him. Some people do hate him, you know. You don't hate him, do you, Jane . . . ? No, you're his only real friends. Oh, Jane! Isn't life cruel? He could have done anything. I've held him back somehow, I don't know how. I've held him down.

JANE. He loves you, Sheila.

SHEILA. I should have gone off and had the baby on my own. I could have coped then. I wasn't always like this, Jane! Because he's pulled me down, too! And then I think, perhaps I *want* him to go. Maybe that's why I keep thinking about it. Maybe that's why I'm so frightened of it.

JANE. Sheila, he loves you. I know he does.

SHEILA. Yes, well . . . Are *you* happy, Jane?

JANE. Oh, don't worry about me.

SHEILA. *I* think you're happy. Aren't you?

JANE. Heavens, I don't know. I'm not sure I've ever stopped to consider it.

SHEILA. You must be!

JANE. Must I?

SHEILA. Someone's got to be happy! It doesn't make sense otherwise. I just stand there in the kitchen sometimes and hold on to the table and think, Well, *Jane*'s happy, at any rate.

JANE. You'll be happy again. I promise you.

SHEILA. *Are* you happy, Jane?

JANE. I've been very lucky. I realise that.

SHEILA. You won't say it, will you.

JANE. Sheila, love, it's not something you can *ask* anyone to say.

SHEILA. Nobody will ever say it. Sometimes I think it's because they're frightened to admit it. And then sometimes I think it's because no one is.

JANE. You know what, Sheila? We must get you out of that house during the day. You're going a bit mad over there. We must find you a job. Now, come on, I'll drive you down to the shops and you can get something amazing to give Colin for dinner . . . Where are my keys?

Exit SHEILA *centre.*

What else could I have done? The last thing I wanted was to get involved in Sheila's troubles. I just didn't have any choice! I couldn't have covered my ears! I didn't have much choice about the job I found her, either. I only knew one employer in those days.

Enter DAVID *left.*

DAVID. Work for *me*? Sheila?

JANE. Two or three hours a day, that's all.

DAVID. Doing what?

JANE. Doing all the things *I* do for you. Phone. Letters. Filing . . .

DAVID. So what would you be doing?

JANE. I could spend more time down at Basuto Road.

DAVID. There's less and less you can do there now.

JANE. There's more and more! There's that woman who's being evicted. There's that couple I promised to take down to Ashford to see their son. They'll never go if I don't drive them.

DAVID. No good asking you to help me. You go off and help everyone else in the world instead.

JANE. I don't want to help anyone. I hate helping people. I want to study them. I'm an anthropologist, not a social worker.

DAVID. You'll have to learn to cross over the road sometimes.

JANE. You cross over the road so as not to see one victim and you step on another.

DAVID. Jane, I'm really under pressure.

JANE. Yes, you need more help.

DAVID. Don't you want to help me?

JANE. Not forever. I've always said that. I'm not a secretary.

DAVID. *She's* not a secretary. She's a nurse.

JANE. You need a nurse.

DAVID. Oh, Jane. You know what I love? I love dropping in at the house in the middle of the day, and there you are.

JANE. I hear your step in the hall, and my heart leaps.

DAVID. When I worked at home — that was the best time. When we both worked in the same room all day, because there wasn't anywhere else. Or anyone else. That was the best time of all.

JANE. Things have to change, though, love.

DAVID. Do they?

JANE. That's your profession, isn't it, changing things?

DAVID. My absurd and foolish profession.

JANE. And when you think about poor Colin and Sheila . . .

DAVID. I suppose we still live in one room, by comparison.

JANE. Anyway, it'll only be for a couple of hours a day. You'll hardly see her.

DAVID. Do we have to?

JANE. That's what the children always ask.

DAVID. And do we?

JANE. Yes, we do.

DAVID. What the children always ask then is, Why do we have to?

JANE. And what we always answer is, Because you do.

    Enter SHEILA *right.*

DAVID. I'm only going to pay her what I'd pay anybody.

JANE. Oh, love, she'll be so thrilled.

    Exit DAVID *left.*

SHEILA. Work for *David*? Me? Oh, Jane, no, no, no.

JANE. David would be so thrilled if you would.

SHEILA. Jane, I couldn't! I haven't touched a typewriter since I was at school. I'd get in such a muddle. I'd be terrified.

JANE. It's only for David.

SHEILA. I'm terrified of David!

JANE. Sheila!

SHEILA. I am! I don't think you understand what it's like for me. I used to be terrified of you.

JANE. I should have thought David and I were very tame after Colin.

SHEILA. Yes, then there's Colin. What would Colin say?

JANE. It wouldn't affect him. He'd be out at work. So would David, so would I. You could just sit here and have the house to yourself.

SHEILA. Oh, Jane, what's he going to say?

    Enter COLIN *right.*

COLIN. How much is he paying you?

SHEILA. Paying me? Oh, we didn't . . . I didn't ask.

COLIN. He is proposing to pay you?

SHEILA. Oh, yes. I think so. I suppose so.

COLIN. Because your qualifications make you quite a catch for the job. You are a State Registered Nurse.

Exit JANE *left.*

SHEILA. So I'll say yes, shall I?

COLIN. As long as you're not doing it out of charity, my pet. As long as you're not just helping her to get out of the house because he's so beastly to her and she's going mad cooped up on her own all day.

SHEILA. Anyway, I'll try it for a week or two, shall I?

COLIN. I shall expect you to come home each day with a wonderful fund of David-and-Jane stories.

SHEILA. All right. If you think I should.

Exit SHEILA *right.*

Enter DAVID *centre.*

DAVID. I don't believe it! They couldn't do this to me! I think in this one small area of South London they have now finally managed to stamp out the practice of architecture!

SHEILA (*off*). Hoo-hoo!

DAVID. Come in.

Enter SHEILA *centre.*

Exit COLIN *right.*

There's no need to say hoo-hoo. This is where you work now.

SHEILA. Sorry. I thought you were talking to someone.

DAVID. I was. I was talking to myself. They've now scheduled part of the site as a public open space. I give up. I really do. Anyway, you're in charge. The house is yours. Jane's out. I'm just going . . . I'll have to go to eighteen stories . . . Sorry. Letters — on the machine. You know how to use one of these things? Articles, catalogues — I've marked them for filing. Coffee, food — you know where it is — help yourself. Oh, and would you pay the milkman?

Exit DAVID *centre.*

SHEILA. Now . . . Machine . . . Typing paper — where's the

typing paper? I don't know where they keep the typing paper!
No typing paper! No *typewriter* . . . ! (*Into phone.*) Hello . . . ?
No, I'm not, she's not here, I'm just someone who, I've just
come to . . . His secretary . . . ? No, there isn't, well I suppose
I'm well, not really . . . Oh . . . (*She puts the phone down.*)
Where was I? Typewriter! Where do they keep the typewriter
. . . ? (*Into phone.*) Hello . . . ? He's not here . . . I'm sort of
his, I'm his secretary . . . Did he get a letter from you this
morning? I don't know, I haven't seen the, I don't know what
letters, I don't . . . Well, yes, I don't know where he keeps his
engagement diary. Could you ring back when . . . ? Oh . . .
(*Puts phone down.*) Oh God. Oh *God* . . . ! (*Into phone.*)
Hello . . . ? No, she's not here . . . No, Daisy's at school. I'm
David's sort of secretary. I mean Mr Kitzinger's sort of . . .
Sorry . . . ? You were just what . . . ? Laughing, oh, yes . . .
Yes, I'll tell him. Bernie who . . . ?

JANE (*off*). It's only me.

SHEILA. Sorry — I missed that . . . Cousins. Mr Cousins, right . . .

Enter JANE *centre.*

JANE. Just looking in to see how you're getting on.

SHEILA. Mrs Kitzinger's here now if you want to . . . Oh, he's
rung off.

JANE. Who was that?

SHEILA. That was Mr Cousins. Bernie Cousins. In Romford.

JANE. Oh, *Bernie.* His cousin . . . Come on, Sheila, love. Don't
give way. You're doing fine. Didn't David tell you who might
call? Oh, he *is* hopeless. He's no imagination about other
people at all. Come on, I'll make you a list of everyone in his
office — all the people who might call about the jobs in hand
— all his relatives — all my relatives. You're going to be the
best-organised secretary in the business . . . Here are the
tissues, look . . . (*Into phone.*) Hello . . . ? I'll take this — you
make us some coffee . . .

Enter DAVID *left.*

DAVID. 'Thank you for your kind and thoughtful litter . . . I
shall indeed be seeking to reduce the provision for barking —

space . . . ' Still, she's quick to learn. She's got everyone's name straight already.

JANE. I expect you helped her a bit, didn't you?

DAVID. Not really. She also reminded me about my sister's wedding anniversary.

JANE. I wonder how she knew about that.

DAVID. No idea. Did she tell you?

JANE. Did she . . . what?

DAVID. I told her to tell you. You always forget to send my sister a card.

JANE *and* DAVID *go off left.*

SHEILA. It's funny. I never thought about Colin while I was over at the Kitzingers'. I didn't even think much about Matt or Lizzie. Isn't that awful? Not even when I found I could do everything after all. Or even when I found there wasn't all that much to do. Some mornings there was nothing at all. I'd creep out of the kitchen and look into the other rooms. I'd go right through the house, very softly, just opening all the doors, and looking into each room in turn. The children's bedrooms. The bathroom. I'd go into David and Jane's room and very gently slide open the drawers. Not touch anything. Just look. Crisp folded sheets; soft folded shirts; shiny folded slips. And up out of each drawer would come the fresh tidy smell of clean clothes. And the only sound would be the quiet ticking of the clock on the table by their bed. I know people look at me and think, what a misery she is! But I can be happy. I have been happy. I was happy then. I'd go downstairs and find ironing waiting to be done in the basket on top of the washing-machine, and I'd get out the iron and do it. There'd be a whole mountain of stuff waiting at home, and I'd be over at the Kitzingers', doing theirs! Isn't that awful? But there was more time there. Isn't that absurd? Then David would come flying in — or Jane — or both of them.

Enter DAVID *centre.*

DAVID. Sheila, love, it's early closing. Could you possibly run down to the cleaners and fetch my grey suit?

SHEILA. Suit, right. And Mr Harding rang. I pretended not to know what Mr Perry had told the Chairman of the Housing Committee. Was that right?

DAVID. Perfect. Brilliant. Tell Jane I've gone to County Hall.

Exit DAVID *centre.*

SHEILA. Don't forget you're seeing Mr Judd at four.

Enter JANE *left.*

JANE. Sheila, love, could you be an absolute angel? Could you stay on and give the children their tea?

SHEILA. I'd love to.

JANE. I've got to take Mrs Peck in for a big showdown with the Housing Officer.

SHEILA. David's gone to County Hall.

JANE. I can't find my car keys. Where do we keep the spare ones?

SHEILA. On top of the fridge. In the Oxo tin.

JANE. How did we ever survive without you?

Exit JANE *centre.*

SHEILA. And after I'd collected Lizzie at three I'd come back and give the children their tea. All five of them — Matt and Lizzie as well — all round the table together. And I wouldn't just get a packet of fish fingers out of the freezer. I'd make them toad in the hole, or I'd fry up all the leftovers into some great concoction of my own. And little Poppy's eyes would light up, and even Jake once said, 'That was great, Sheila.' And I'd sit there at the head of the table, being Mum, making them wash their hands and lay and clear, and I'd feel so pleased with myself. Isn't it . . . I don't know . . . pathetic, I suppose.

Enter COLIN *right.*

Then I'd have to go back and cook dinner for Colin.

COLIN. I must say, that steak and kidney pie was a triumph. Even with the crust beginning to char, the centre was still frozen. Steak and kidney Alaska.

SHEILA. I'm sorry — I couldn't get back any earlier. David came

home from this meeting and he was in a great state about it.
You know how he gets. Apparently the planning department
are being absolutely rigid about daylight angles.

COLIN. What was that girl in Ibsen called?

SHEILA. What?

COLIN. The one who made the old boy climb up the scaffolding?

SHEILA. No, but it means he can't put a five storey slab along the
railway.

COLIN. Inspired by her youth and vitality, he climbed to the top
of his new high-rise.

SHEILA. No, but that means he can't meet the Yardstick with the
point blocks at eighteen stories.

COLIN. And fell off and broke his neck.

SHEILA. I'm not going to give it up, you know. I'm not. You've
taken everything else away from me. You've laughed me out
of everything I ever had. But not this! I'll fight you about this!
I will, Colin! I'll fight you! I'll fight you!

COLIN. Apricots.

SHEILA. What?

COLIN. I'll have a tin of apricots.

SHEILA. Pears or raspberries. There aren't any apricots.

COLIN *and* SHEILA *go off right.*

Enter DAVID *centre.*

DAVID. Right. Site plan. Sketch pad. Pencils . . . Peace. Quiet . . .
Let architecture commence. Forty whole minutes — thirty-five
whole minutes — of actual architecture . . . Now, where are
we? Six eighteen-storey blocks . . . Can't go there — cable.
Can't go there . . . overshadowing. Can't go there, because then
the vehicular access has to go *there*, and that's within fifty
metres of the junction. Start again. Five twenty-four storey
blocks . . . Not losing any units . . . ? Gaining forty-eight units.
Right. Six extra stories, so they'll have to go back how far?
Where are the daylight protractors . . . ? Hold on. Now I'm

overshadowing the low-rise . . . ! Oh, it's such a battle! I can't fight shut up in this little kitchen . . . ! Sheila!

Enter SHEILA *left.*

SHEILA. Sorry.

DAVID. I thought you'd gone home.

SHEILA. I was upstairs.

DAVID. Talking to myself, was I?

SHEILA. It's lovely seeing you work.

DAVID. I can't work.

SHEILA. I won't disturb you. I've got to go out and get Lizzie, you see.

DAVID. I couldn't work in the office. I can't work here . . . I think I'll walk round the block . . . Lizzie?

SHEILA. It's three o'clock. I've got to fetch her from school.

Exit SHEILA *centre.*

DAVID. Hold on. I'll come with you. Anything's better than working.

Exit DAVID *centre.*

Enter SHEILA *right.*

SHEILA. That's why we first went for a walk together — to fetch Lizzie. Funny, when you think about it. After that we went to the park two or three times. Once or twice we went as far as the woods. Sometimes he'd talk about Basuto Road, or one of his other schemes. Sometimes he'd just mooch along in silence, with his hands in his pockets and his shoulders hunched up, scuffing his feet through the piles of fallen leaves like a boy coming home from school.

Enter COLIN *left.*

Once in the woods a leaf came spinning slowly down from the bare branches right in front of me. I've chased after falling leaves with the children sometimes; I can never catch them. But this one — I just opened my hand, and it settled like a bird. A year's happiness.

Exit SHEILA *right.*

JANE (*off*). Hello! It's only me!

Enter JANE *centre.*

I've been sitting in that damned hospital with the Swain boy for nearly two hours . . . Colin! I thought you were Sheila!

COLIN. I found some fish fingers in the fridge. I gave the children those. They're upstairs watching television.

JANE. Funny to see you sitting at the kitchen table again. You haven't been for ages.

COLIN. No.

JANE. How long have you been here?

COLIN. Most of the afternoon.

JANE. Where's Sheila?

COLIN. Where indeed? The school rang at half-past three to say that Lizzie was still standing outside the gates.

JANE. I'm sorry, Colin. I know what you feel about Sheila working here.

COLIN. Do you?

JANE. Have you asked David where she is?

COLIN. No.

JANE. Isn't he here?

COLIN. No.

JANE. I'll ring the office.

COLIN. The office say he's here.

JANE. His stuff's here.

COLIN. So I observe.

JANE. I expect they've gone for a walk, then.

COLIN. Gone for a walk?

JANE. David likes to wander round the neighbourhood when he's brooding about a scheme. I think Sheila sometimes tags on.

COLIN. Taking dictation as they go?

JANE. I don't suppose David says very much. He just likes to have someone there.

COLIN. So they're walking about the neighbourhood in silence. For three hours. In the rain.

JANE. Taken shelter. Gone to the pictures. *I* don't know.

COLIN. You know she's in love with him?

JANE. Colin. Dear Colin . . .

COLIN. Not news to you, I'm sure.

JANE. News. That's right. That's just what it is — news. David says he doesn't know how you became a journalist. I know. Because that's your trade. You look as if you don't care what anyone thinks, but you do, you care a lot, you want us all to be surprised and shocked, you want to get a reaction.

COLIN. Got a reaction this time, anyway.

JANE. Yes. I'm sorry. But it makes me angry, Colin, when you talk like that. David wants everyone to love him . . .

COLIN. And apparently everyone does.

JANE. . . . And you want everyone to hate you. Or perhaps you don't. Perhaps you want to test them. You want them to love you in spite of being hateful.

COLIN. Don't worry, Jane. I don't suppose he's in love with her.

JANE. If you want to know the truth, she's frightened of him.

COLIN. Of course. She's frightened of you, too.

JANE. She used to be.

COLIN. She used to be in love with you.

JANE. You are a fool, you know, Colin. You only get one life. You can't go back and say, Please, Miss, I've spoilt this one, can I have another?

COLIN. A twinge of jealousy there, I thought. Just for an instant. Odd how reflexive it is. I'm sure you weren't in love with her.

JANE. You always want to pull everyone down. You pull her down. That's what makes her so insecure.

COLIN. Why, what did she say to you?

JANE. Nothing. She doesn't need to say anything.

COLIN. Did she say, 'Jane, I think he's going to leave me'? Did she . . . ? I see she did.

JANE. *Are* you going to leave her?

COLIN. Jane, I have a quiet laugh sometimes when I think about you going down there to Basutoland and helping people. In fact we both have a quiet laugh about it. I can still make her laugh, you know. About you and David, at any rate. You and David are a great force in keeping us together. Because I can't imagine what you make of the Basutos. You don't seem to understand the plain, everyday folk across the street. You haven't grasped one basic general principle — that other people's lives are at least as complicated as your own. At least as dense and extraordinary. And just as unlike your life as your life is unlike theirs.

JANE. You haven't answered my question.

COLIN. I am answering it. Sheila and I have been through all this business before, you see. The falling in love. The running across the road. The 'Help me, help me.' The 'I'm going mad.' The 'Oh God, he's going to leave me.' Last time it was a couple of music teachers. This is when we were living in that flat, before you kindly found us the house. She started with Mrs. Got Mrs driving her everywhere, giving her meals, looking after the baby. Then she announced that she wanted to take up singing. Mrs taught singing. Give her an interest, take her out of herself. So for six months she had singing lessons. Practised, too. An hour a day, without fail. Have you heard Sheila singing . . . ? Then she said she wanted to learn the oboe. Mr taught the oboe. And she would have done it, too, Jane! She would have practised the oboe!

JANE. Poor Sheila.

COLIN. She's tone-deaf.

JANE. So you stopped her?

COLIN. I had a word with Mrs. Life goes round like a wheel, Jane. What we've done once we do again. Round and round.

We don't change. We never escape.

JANE. She may not be good at music, but she's good at helping David and me. So that's a change from last time.

COLIN. Good, is she? What, efficient? Well-organised?

JANE. I don't know what we'd do without her.

COLIN. I can believe that, as a matter of fact. How absurd things are.

JANE. I hope she'll go on working here. So that's another change from last time. And *are* you going to leave her?

COLIN. She used to be frightened of me once, of course. She used to be in love with me. I've got to have one stick left in the rack.

JANE. That you?

DAVID (*off*). Only me.

Enter DAVID *and* SHEILA *centre*.

DAVID. Only us . . . Colin!

SHEILA. What are you doing here?

DAVID. We got caught in the rush-hour.

SHEILA. Where are the children? *Where's Lizzie?*

COLIN. Standing outside the school, I presume.

JANE. She's upstairs, watching television. They're both upstairs.

DAVID. We got caught in the rain.

SHEILA. Didn't they get my message?

DAVID. So we found a teashop and had four lots of tea.

SHEILA. I rang the school! I told them to tell Lizzie to come home with Matt! Upstairs . . . ?

Exit SHEILA *left*.

DAVID. Then we got caught in the rush-hour . . . You're not going? Stay for supper. We haven't seen you for months . . .

Exit COLIN *centre*.

Have a drink . . . I'll open some wine . . .

Exit DAVID *centre.*

Enter SHEILA *right.*

SHEILA. Early in the new year, that was. Cold. Wet. A terrible start to a terrible year. Why do I say that? Amazing things happened that year! I wouldn't go through that year again . . . Lizzie never got my message for one very simple reason. I never sent it. I was lying. I'd forgotten all about her. Isn't that awful? I mean truly awful . . . As soon as I came into the kitchen and saw Colin and Jane sitting at the table like that I knew that he'd been telling her. And yes, I was in love with David. And no, I was never in love with the oboe-teacher, nor with the oboe-teacher's wife, nor with the man at the estate-agent's. Or perhaps he didn't tell her about that. I don't think even Colin believed that one. But he had this idea that nothing changes, that nothing ever can be changed. This is what kept him going, thinking that he understood this, and no one else did. And when he lifted his eyes like that and looked at you . . . when he half-lifted his eyes and half-looked at you . . . then you knew it was true. You felt hypnotised. You *couldn't* do anything . . . But it's true that I was in love with David. And that it was absurd, now the words had been said, now the thought had been thought. Absurd and painful and humiliating. Because David certainly wasn't in love with me. Why should he have been? No one has ever been in love with me, except Colin, for three months by that lake in Switzerland and one month back in London afterwards. I don't really know what David thought about me. I wasn't with him all that often, and he didn't say much when we were. I think he quite liked me being round the house. He'd have preferred Jane. Or the children. But I was better than no one. That's how I was the first to hear about the skyscrapers. He walked into the kitchen while I was working at the table, and stood looking out of the window with his hands in his pockets, laughing to himself. He had to tell someone. And I was there.

JANE. Colin was right, of course. She *was* a bit in love with David. And, yes, I suppose she'd had some kind of silly crush on me all the previous summer. And with Jake and Daisy and Poppy, for that matter. Poor Sheila. But fancy forgetting to pick

Lizzie up! I didn't believe that story about phoning the school.
I think she was gazing up at David somewhere and she forgot.
Poor silly Sheila. I wonder if she realised she was in love with
him. I don't think David did. I couldn't tell him, of course.
He'd have had to stop her coming to the house. As long as
they didn't know — as long as they didn't hear it put into
words — we could all just about get by. Or perhaps he did
know.

Enter DAVID *centre.*

I look at him from so much further off these days. I see all
kinds of things I didn't see then. Perhaps he did know. He was
never in love with her, I'm certain of that, not at any time, not
for a moment. But perhaps he knew that some kind of tribute
was being laid at his feet. Perhaps he thought it was no more
than he was entitled to. He certainly liked having someone
around to talk to about his work. He told her some things
before he told me. He told her about the skyscrapers. How
could he have been such a fool?

Exit JANE *left.*

DAVID. Skyscrapers, Sheila. That's the answer. That's the *only*
answer. I've tried every other solution, and it doesn't work.
I'm going to build 150 low-rise walk-ups for families with
young children, and then 600 units for all the rest in twin
skyscrapers. What do you think? I don't mean eleven stories,
or eighteen, or twenty-four. I mean fifty stories. The highest
residential buildings in Europe. What do you think? I've just
come from a long meeting with the structural engineers, and
it can be done. There'll be endless problems, there'll be endless
objections, but I'm going to do it, Sheila. Because in the end
it's not art — it's mathematics. A simple equation. You collect
up the terms, you get rid of the brackets, you replace all the
a's and b's with the number of three-person households and
the length of a coffin and the turning-circle of a corporation
refuse vehicle — and there at the bottom of the page on the
righthand side is the answer; 150 low-rise walk-ups and two
socking great skyscrapers. I feel dizzy just thinking about
them. When the clouds are low they'll be lost in cloud. On
misty still November mornings they'll be *above* the clouds.

When it's clear you'll be able to see the whole length of the North Downs, from Hampshire into Kent. You'll be able to see the Thames Valley one way and the Thames Estuary the other. What do you think? They'll be a hazard to aircraft, Sheila! So what do you think? Half of South London's going to be in their rain-shadow! They'll change the whole climate! I'm joking, Sheila, I'm joking. I'm just shouting and jumping up and down a bit before the bell goes and I'm back in class again. Do you realise you'll be able to stand on the Chilterns and see my skyscrapers over the top of Hampstead Heath! Won't you? Where's the map? In the office. Back at six.

Exit DAVID *centre.*

Enter COLIN *right.*

COLIN. Sheila, my love, I've poured you a small glass of the whisky you gave me for Christmas. We're not dead yet, Sheila. We can still enjoy ourselves from time to time. We can still have a laugh together.

SHEILA. But why is it so funny, if it's the only way he can do it?

COLIN. To all low-flying aircraft in the vicinity of SE15.

SHEILA. But if it's going to give people a good view . . .

COLIN. To a more abundant rainfall on the plains of Basutoland.

SHEILA. I suppose it is a bit funny, after everything he's said.

COLIN. To bed, then, my love. And to David, who does what he can to bring the semi-detached a little closer together.

COLIN *and* SHEILA *go off right.*

Enter JANE *centre.*

JANE. It's only the evening paper. I thought you'd better see it, though.

Enter DAVID *centre.*

Where did they get the story? That's what I don't understand.

DAVID. 'Residents in South-east London spoke out today against plans to build New York-style skyscrapers as part of a local council redevelopment scheme . . . ' Plans? What plans? I haven't even done the outline proposals yet! I haven't set pen to paper! 'The two skyscrapers would be the highest residential buildings in Europe . . . ' I haven't told anyone apart from you! ' "No one has consulted us," said old-age pensioner Mr William Pavey . . . ' Of course no one's consulted them! There's nothing to consult them about yet! 'The skyscrapers would be visible from as far away as the South Downs . . . ' Everything wrong, as usual. 'There are fears that they could be a hazard to aircraft, and they could even affect South London's weather . . .' Oh my God.

JANE. You told Sheila?

DAVID. I told Sheila.

JANE. She'll have to go, David.

DAVID. She can't possibly have picked up the phone and rung the newspapers!

JANE. No, it would have been Colin who told the newspapers.

DAVID. What, picked up the phone . . . ?

JANE. Talked to someone somewhere. It's his profession! And then he's jealous of you. He's always been jealous of you.

SHEILA (*off*). Hoo-hoo!

JANE. And she colludes with him. She buys him off by feeding him amusing little titbits about you and me. She sells us to him! I know how they work, those two!

SHEILA. Hoo-hoo!

JANE. She'll destroy you, David. She'll destroy us both. You'll have to tell her. Now! While the paper's still in your hand!

Enter SHEILA *centre.*

SHEILA. It's me . . . Sorry . . . I've got the children — we've got cases and bags . . . Oh, Jane! I've left him!

JANE. Bring the children in, then, Sheila.

DAVID. I'll get the bags.

SHEILA *and* DAVID *go off centre.*

JANE. They looked like two little refugees. All white faces and wide eyes. They cheered up, though. They watched television, they played pelmanism all over the floor with Poppy, and Poppy let them win. Then they drank their cocoa and went to bed as if they'd always lived in our house. Which of course they pretty much had. Sheila was a rather more difficult case. Well, obviously. She kept saying she couldn't possibly stay, so could we drive her to a hotel. She made us lock the front door and promise not to let Colin in. She couldn't eat. Then after we'd washed up and put everything away she suddenly felt weak and dizzy with hunger. She cried a bit. She also laughed a bit.

Enter SHEILA *centre.*

She kept saying it seemed so normal sitting at our kitchen table. Which of course it was. And she couldn't stop saying how awful she felt about letting David down.

Enter DAVID *centre.*

SHEILA. The phone went, and as soon as he said he was from the newspapers I knew what had happened. It was like one of those dreams where you just suddenly know this awful thing has gone wrong. He asked to speak to you — I said you were out all afternoon. So he said, could I help him because they'd heard this report that you were designing two skyscrapers in the path of aircraft coming into London Airport.

DAVID. It's not important, Sheila. It won't make any difference. All my fault for saying anything.

SHEILA. Well, I panicked. I just put the phone down. It rang again. I picked it up and it was the same man, so I just put it down again without saying anything. I suppose that must have made it seem worse. But I couldn't think what to do. All I could think was, This is Colin! Colin did this to me!

DAVID. Skyscrapers. That was a joke, too, calling them skyscrapers.

SHEILA. When he came in last night I didn't say anything. But I could see from the way he looked at me. He knew I'd found out. I felt as if a mouthful of scalding coffee was going down my throat. I've been sitting here all day today thinking about it. I won't let him take this away from me! I won't! I won't! So then I went back to get his dinner, and I took the remains of yesterday's stew out of the fridge, and I saw him sitting there at the table, looking at me, and I could smell the stew, and it was cold and brown, all cold and brown, and I suppose I threw it at him, because I was shaking and sobbing and there was this foul brown stuff all over everything.

JANE. She went to bed eventually.

DAVID. You've got everything you need? Anything you want, Sheila, just tell us.

Exit SHEILA *left.*

JANE. David and I stayed up for another hour or more, talking about it. Or not talking about it. We'd started to feel uneasy about Colin by this time.

DAVID. We should have given him a ring and told him they were all right.

JANE. It's after midnight now.

DAVID. I suppose he's going to think this is all our doing.

JANE. Well, it isn't.

DAVID. Isn't it?

JANE. David, we did everything we could to help them. We did. Both of us. We truly and sincerely did.

DAVID. Yes. If we *hadn't* tried to help them they'd still be together. Perhaps I should go round. What do you think?

JANE. We rang him in the morning. There was no reply. We rang him in the evening. We rang him next day, and the next. Then his office rang us; he hadn't been in all week. And I suddenly remembered something I'd half-noticed. I went outside and looked across the road at their windows; I was right. I can feel even now that slow wave of cold spreading up from my stomach, shrinking the skin on my face, then the scalp over my head. The curtains were still drawn; they'd been drawn all week. He couldn't have done! Not Colin. He didn't hate himself enough for that. He didn't hate Sheila enough . . .

Enter SHEILA *left.*

I didn't say anything to her. I just quietly took their spare key out of the tin on the refrigerator, and went across the road. I didn't run. I walked. I unlocked their front door quite calmly, thinking nothing, keeping my head quite empty . . . It was a kind of brown twilight behind the curtains inside. There were children's toys underfoot, and overturned cardboard boxes. I opened the living-room door, and there was the life they'd shared, abandoned at one muddled arbitrary moment in time. Clothes waiting to be mended; more toys; open newspapers; two unwashed nursery mugs. Everything gone cold and still . . . I opened the kitchen door, and there it was — the unmistakeable stench of putrefying flesh . . . Funny, when I look back on it. I'd worked out what it was by the time I opened the door again. It was just like Sheila had said — foul and brown and everywhere. But it *was* me who found him in the end. In a derelict house in Frances Road, in the middle of David's redevelopment area. The council had just started to move people out. I saw this front door standing ajar, and I pushed it open. I don't know why. I suppose I thought there might be something bad inside. And there he was.

Enter COLIN *centre.*

COLIN. Come in. Welcome to the war.

Curtain.

ACT TWO

The same.

DAVID

DAVID. Basuto Road. Those sour stale words. You look up from your work, and there they are along the files. Or you're going down some other path in your mind altogether — and suddenly they're coming towards you. The same shabby sad-eyed pair. And before you know what you're doing you've turned and crossed the street to avoid them. Why? What could they say that hasn't been said?

Enter JANE *and* SHEILA *centre.*

SHEILA. In Basuto Road?

JANE. In Frances Road, to be precise.

DAVID. After all, the Basuto Road scheme included our very successful redevelopment of Colin and Sheila. We should have had awards for our work on them, we should have had bronze plaques to put up.

SHEILA. 'Welcome to the war'? What war?

JANE. Against the scheme.

DAVID. I mean that. Jane used to say that when she opened the front door in Frances Road she didn't recognise him for a moment. He seemed taller. His eyes were fully open. He was alive. And I say, good for him.

SHEILA. And he's *living* there? He's got himself a flat on David's site?

JANE. It's a squat.

SHEILA. A *squat*?

JANE. The council have started clearing the houses. As the tenants move out so the squatters move in.

DAVID. And I wouldn't have recognised Sheila when she heard the news. All of a sudden she was — well, yes, she was *alive*. And I say, good for her.

SHEILA. What sort of squatters?

JANE. I don't know. Young people.

SHEILA. Colin hates young people.

JANE. Rather tired old young people, so far as I could see.

SHEILA. He hates old people. He hates everyone.

JANE. They've got electricity and water, and one or two bits of furniture. It's not too bad.

SHEILA. I don't care if it is too bad. I hope it's terrible. I hope he's infested with lice.

DAVID. No, if we still had offices I'd put up photographs of Colin and Sheila in reception. The sort that architectural photographers take through ultra-violet filters. Dreamlike white sunlit shapes towering against black skies full of summer clouds. Perhaps Sheila would be the low-rise part of the development, the family walk-ups. But Colin . . . Colin would be towering.

SHEILA. He's gone mad! What does he think he's doing?

JANE. Organising a campaign against the scheme.

SHEILA. Organising a campaign? How can he organise a campaign? He can't even organise his own children!

JANE. Well, he's organised all this lot out of their sleeping bags.

SHEILA. He's never lifted a finger for them!

JANE. He's got them all painting posters.

SHEILA. He can't organise himself!

JANE. They were all smoking animatedly.

DAVID. A twilight area. That's what Colin and Sheila were when we started work on them. They were like Basuto Road — full of hidden sewers and geological faults. We got them stood up in the sunshine. They fell down again later, of course, the way some buildings of the period did. But that wasn't the design —

that was defective materials. No, seriously, we helped them, we did them some good. I haven't done all that much good in this world, it seems. But I did give Colin and Sheila a purpose in life. In fact I gave them two. I gave them one each.

SHEILA. You don't know what he's like! He's hopeless! He can't even do his job properly! They'll be ringing up again — I know they will! He'll be sacked! He's been sacked before!

JANE. He won't be this time, Sheila. He's resigned.

SHEILA. I knew it! I knew he would, sooner or later! What are we going to live on? Has he forgotten he's got a family to support?

DAVID. Sheila, love, don't worry, don't get upset. You can always rely on us. You know that.

SHEILA. You don't understand what he's like! He comes here and smiles and you think he's someone like you. But he's not. He's evil. All he can do is to pull down and destroy. He hates you. You don't understand what that is, someone hating you. He's going to pull you down and destroy your scheme. I know he is! He's destroyed me, and now he's going to destroy you. I'm nothing. I don't count in his eyes. But he's used me to get at you. That's what I shall never forgive myself.

SHEILA *and* JANE *go off left.*

DAVID. She kept coming back to that all evening. That and the money. That and the money and how she couldn't go on staying with us now she'd let us down like this and how she couldn't afford to live anywhere now there was no money. We didn't get her to bed until one o'clock. Then we sat up talking to each other. It was the only time we were ever alone together.

Enter JANE *left.*

JANE. She's still in a great state.

DAVID. Was that all right, saying she could work full time? I thought it might make her worry less about the money.

JANE. Funny, though, isn't it. You're supporting Colin's family so that he's free to destroy your livelihood.

DAVID. Not much he can do, really.

JANE. Isn't there?

DAVID. Well, is there? I don't think the Housing Committee's going to pay much attention to some wretched squatter. Is he all right down there?

JANE. Having the time of his life, so far as I could see.

DAVID. Is there anything we can do for him, do you think?

JANE. You mean, *help* him?

DAVID. We're helping Sheila. We don't want to take sides.

JANE. David, sides have been taken! Colin's taken them! Whatever side we're on, he's on the opposite one!

DAVID. He's still a friend.

JANE. No, he's not — he's an enemy!

DAVID. Look, he may have decided he hates us — I don't know — but we don't have to hate him back.

JANE. Sheila's right — you don't understand what it is, being hated. You think everyone else in the world is like yourself . . . I suppose that's what Colin said about me.

DAVID. Be no good if I went to see him? What do you think?

JANE. It's not a virtue, David. It's a sort of moral blindness.

DAVID. Or if *you* went back?

JANE. I'm not going anywhere near him. I feel the same as Sheila. I hope he starves. I hope he's eaten by rats.

Exit JANE *left*.

DAVID. They all took it so personally! Even Jane. The blood rose to her cheeks, her eyes sparkled. The Basuto Wars had started. My wars, of course, but I still felt like a bemused neutral observer. I didn't understand Colin's feelings. But then I'd never understood anything about him, from the first moment I'd met him. I didn't think he was driven by jealousy, or bitterness that we'd broken up his marriage. I thought really he was against the scheme because he was against the scheme. Why shouldn't he be against it? Why shouldn't he try and stop it? It's a free country, and anyway there was nothing he could do. That's how it seemed to me. That's how it seemed to me then, I suppose. Where had we got to by that stage? I finished the outline proposals in July. That must have been April. Well, early days.

Exit DAVID *left.*

Enter COLIN *right.*

COLIN. May. The beginning of May. I'd wake soon after five each morning, when it started to get light, because of course there were no curtains at the window. I'd feel the slippery nylon of the sleeping-bag around me, and the narrow canvas of the camp-bed, and I'd remember where I was. I'd look round the room. One suitcase of clean clothes; a single wooden chair; a few books on the shelf in the corner. Nothing else. Bare boards, bare walls. And I'd feel a lightness, a physical lightness. I'd laugh sometimes for sheer physical pleasure. Though there were times when I wept. That was for the children. For their endless colds and their nagging coughs, for their desolate vomitings and helpless retchings, for the feel of them sitting in my lap wrapped in eiderdowns, with hot muddled aching heads leaning against my chest. Always ill. But if you're a nurse, like Sheila, someone has to be a patient. And that would make me think of David, and I'd laugh again. Sooner or later he'd be coming to see me, full of concern. Concerned about Sheila, of course — even more concerned about me. Perhaps just a little concerned about his scheme. He'd look all hurt and puzzled. He'd want to know why I'd done it. What could I say? Public spirit? Jealousy? Pique? I didn't know why I'd done it! Perhaps just to see the look on his face when he came to ask me. But I was wrong about that.

Enter JANE *right.*

JANE. Your mail.

COLIN. Jane.

JANE. It's all right. I'm not staying.

COLIN. I thought it would be David.

JANE. I was passing the door.

COLIN. Does David know you're here?

JANE. No.

COLIN. A clandestine meeting.

JANE. Why did you do it, Colin?

COLIN. Why did I do it? I should have guessed it would be you. David looks concerned; you're the one who has to run around and *be* concerned.

JANE. Why did you marry her?

COLIN. Why did I *marry* her?

JANE. It was a cruel thing to do.

COLIN. Leaflets?

JANE. What?

COLIN. Do you want to fold some?

JANE. You won't stop it. You know that. You won't have any effect at all.

COLIN. How are the children?

JANE. *Your* children?

COLIN. Yes, my children.

JANE. All right.

COLIN. How are *your* children, then? How's Sheila? How's David?

JANE. Sheila says you can see the children on Saturday.

COLIN. Perhaps you could drive them over?

JANE. That's not a serious suggestion. I hope.

COLIN. I've no car, Jane. I'm out of work. I'm homeless. I'm one of your Basutos now!

JANE. A squat. So this is what you want, is it, Colin?

COLIN. What do you think I've been living in for the last ten years? Actually it reminds me of school. Bare boards and cold water and smelly feet.

JANE. And a lot of admiring fourth-formers.

COLIN. Yes, and something serious to do.

JANE. Folding leaflets?

COLIN. Another house to beat for the house shield. Someone to defeat. And you want to know why I married Sheila? Out of kindness, Jane. Out of the kindness of my heart. My one crime.

JANE. Colin, can I tell you something I've never told you before? Something I've never said to anyone, ever.

COLIN. A secret.

JANE. Yes, a secret.

COLIN. This is why you've come to see me, is it?

JANE. Possibly.

COLIN. You're in love with me.

JANE. More secret than that. I don't like you.

COLIN. Oh, Jane.

JANE. I never have liked you.

COLIN. Jane, Jane, Jane.

JANE. So now I've said it.

COLIN. After twenty years. Does David know?

JANE. He does now. And what a stupid farce it was, pretending I did like you! Because now you don't even like David! You hate him!

COLIN. I like you, Jane.

JANE. No, you don't.

COLIN. Oh, yes. I like you because I see in you a little of the blackness I have in me. That's why you don't like me. Because you know I can see it.

JANE. Yes. Well.

COLIN. Anyway, you have more hot soup to distribute. I'll tell you another secret, though, Jane. You're the expert on helping the Basutos, and you know the scheme's not going to help them. You loathe it as much as I do. You won't tell David that, of course. Don't worry — I won't tell him. That really is a secret . . . Or do you mean it was even a secret from yourself?

JANE. Saturday — I'll leave the children at the door.

Exit JANE *right.*

Enter DAVID *and* SHEILA *centre.*

DAVID. Where's Jane?

SHEILA. She's gone to see some people in Wandsworth.

DAVID. I still haven't finished the elevations.

SHEILA. I'll wait dinner for her, shall I? It's only stew.

DAVID. They've got to be at the Borough Architect's office in the morning.

SHEILA. I'll take them in.

DAVID. I'm not going to get to bed at all. Wandsworth?

SHEILA. SW something.

DAVID. There. What do you think?

SHEILA. I think it's brilliant, David.

DAVID. How about the new walkways?

SHEILA. They're brilliant. Everything. It's all, I don't know, absolutely . . . well . . .

DAVID. Brilliant, yes, but don't cry, Sheila. It's not that brilliant. Just get the dinner on the table. I'll eat and work at the same time. You know what it's missing, though, Sheila . . . ? Handkerchief . . . One small element in the design? People. No people! Where are the people? Ah, whole packet of people. Very nice class of tenant you get from Letraset. Well-dressed. Don't write on the walls. Don't stuff old mattresses down the rubbish-chutes.

JANE (*off*). Only me.

DAVID. And they don't over-eat. Nothing like fat people for throwing the architecture out of scale.

Enter JANE *centre.*

So what do you think?

JANE. Very good . . . I meant to say use up the cold chicken.

SHEILA. I've made sandwiches with it for the children's lunch.

DAVID. Sheila thinks it's brilliant.

JANE. Spot of grease. You shouldn't work in the kitchen.

DAVID. I'll put someone over it. Actually, you could have fat people standing at the bottom of these things and no one'd ever notice. No one'd ever *see* them . . . What?

JANE. Nothing. Just looking.

DAVID. Has he managed to stir up the Basutos yet?

JANE. I've been over in Wandsworth.

DAVID. Don't worry — it can't possibly affect us. This'll be in front of the Housing Committee tomorrow. With any luck I'll have the full scheme design in front of the council next winter — and that's the first the Basutos will know about it. Suddenly there'll be a huge scale model on display at the Town Hall, with little cars on the roads and lots of trees made out of green loofah . . . What?

JANE. Nothing. Just thinking.

DAVID. I'm telling Sheila. You don't have to listen.

JANE. You're very up today.

DAVID. Up all day. Up all night.

JANE. Up all month.

DAVID. Anyway, Sheila, by the time we get to scheme design it'll be too late, because (a) everyone loves a scale model, and (b) no one's going to notice it's there, and (c) the council will have spent a hundred thousand pounds, and no one's going to persuade them they've spent it all for nothing . . . Jane, don't listen if you don't like it! Don't look! Go and call the children!

JANE. They offered me a job.

DAVID. Who offered you a job?

JANE. These people I've been talking to.

DAVID. What people?

JANE. These people in Wandsworth. It's a kind of housing trust.

DAVID. You've stopped working for me altogether?

JANE. I haven't decided whether to take the job yet.

DAVID. I mean, if it's housing you're interested in, that's what I'm doing — housing. That's what this trust does, is it? It builds houses?

JANE. It preserves houses. It rehabilitates them, so they don't have to be pulled down.

SHEILA. I'll call the children, shall I?

JANE. David, I can't always think the same as you about everything.

DAVID. No. Think what you like. Do what you like. Free country.

SHEILA. I'll get the children.

JANE. *I'll* get them.

Exit JANE *left.*

DAVID. Put another happy little family group on the concourse here, look. Husband walking left, wife walking right.

COLIN. Only one thing I learnt at school turned out to be much use in life, and that was writing Greek hexameters. If you can get some aspect of human destiny into five dactyls and a spondee then you can get the headline on a magazine article into thirty points across two. You can also get a programme of political action on to a piece of cardboard small enough to be held up and waved about in the air. I took real pleasure in the work. 'Don't scrape the skies — just sweep the streets.' A whole philosophy of government in eight syllables. I was rather proud of one that went: 'Fifty stories! And forty nine of them with no foundation.'

DAVID. Amendments. Re-drawings.

SHEILA. Night night.

DAVID. Off to bed.

SHEILA. It's nearly twelve. Don't get up.

Exit SHEILA *centre.*

DAVID. Some of the more half-baked members of the Housing Committee thought the water-garden looked dangerous. Then they thought people might get dizzy if they looked over a balcony with a 450-foot drop underneath it. Been got at by someone, I suppose. Well, why shouldn't he? Free country.

COLIN. We also wrote on lavatory walls. The Town Hall lavatory walls. 'Living in the sky is strictly for the birds.' 'Spread a little sogginess — give a cloud a home.' These were the high-rise slogans, designed to accommodate disaffected social workers. Most of the campaign was rather more low-rise. 'Hands off our homes!' 'Save our streets!' Some of it was lower still. 'Town Hall *Sieg Heil*.' 'Skyscrapers = SS.' We had all kinds of supporters by this time. Not all of them had heads.

DAVID. But the sheer labour of it! This is when the problems with the foundations began to emerge. They'd have to be bigger — we'd have to divert the Generating Board's megavolt cable after all. I'd sit hunched over the drawing-board late into the night, struggling with all the problems, and I couldn't help laughing sometimes. There were people out there in the night somewhere struggling to make the problems harder!

COLIN. But the sheer pleasure of it! We sprayed walls two stories high — 'Vandals out!' We shouted council meetings down — 'Democracy now!' We didn't have to worry about being fair or truthful or tidy. That was the great liberation. Fairness and tidiness and truth are for people who've got what they want already. We had nothing; we could do anything.

DAVID. I felt no resentment for Colin, though. Nothing but sadness. It was like seeing someone destroy himself with drink. Deliberately blunting his own intelligence and feeling. Deliberately dissolving his life in waste and futility.

COLIN. I sometimes thought about David, hunched over his drawing-board far into the night, and I couldn't help laughing. He was using up his life designing a scheme that was never going to be built. That everyone but him knew was never going to be built. That he knew was never going to be built.

DAVID. I could have done with some help from Jane. No, that was unfair. No reason why she should have to work for me if she didn't want to. Better for her to have her own job. And if she was going to start preserving things, better for her to be preserving them over in Wandsworth.

Exit DAVID *left*.

COLIN. I did one fair and tidy thing, though. I suggested the name of an excellent field-worker to our friends in Wandsworth. I gave Jane her start in life, at any rate.

Exit COLIN *right*.

Enter JANE *centre*.

JANE. David not back?

Enter SHEILA *left*.

SHEILA. He's over the road. He's measuring the kitchen. Oh, Jane, I do feel awful about him working on my house when he's so busy already.

JANE. If you're busy you can always do more. It's having too little to do that makes you feel like doing less. Are they washed?

SHEILA. I'm going to fold them.

JANE. I'll help you. Quite funny, really, David doing a rehab. Rehabilitating your house. Why doesn't he pull it down and start again? Why didn't we pull this one down?

SHEILA. It is different, though, isn't it, Jane?

JANE. Is it?

SHEILA. Jane, there are lots of people who haven't got homes at all. We've got to build them *something*. I know you worry about it, Jane, but it's got to be done. You know it has.

JANE. It's like a bonfire, isn't it. Faith, I mean. It flares up here — it dies down there. You never know where or when.

SHEILA. Jane, perhaps I shouldn't say this, but I see you and David every day and I know you don't really agree with what he's doing, and I can't help worrying about it. Because I know what you think. You think we ought to ask people more what they actually want. But, Jane, it's no good asking people what they want, because they don't know what they want until they've got it. No one asked them if they wanted Basuto Road the way it is now. Probably in the first place they didn't! It may have been years before they realised they wanted it like that! People aren't all as clever as you, Jane! *I'm* not! I didn't want to work for David. You made me. And you were right, and I'll be grateful until the day I die!

JANE. This is what David's been telling you?

SHEILA. David doesn't know what people want, but I do, because I know what *I* want. I don't want David to ask me what colour my kitchen should be. I want him to tell me. I don't want him to ask me whether I want the house redesigned. I just want him to do it. And when I say I feel awful about it and he shouldn't be doing it I don't want him *not* to do it! That's what people are like, Jane! That's what most people are like. Colin doesn't know what he wants! I know you feel sorry for him and you take his part — but he doesn't know what he wants any more than I do! Or he didn't, until he saw somebody else who did, and then he knew he wanted to stop it and smash it. Because it's all part of the same old battle between good and evil, the same old war between light and dark. I know you won't like my saying that. But it is, Jane, and you mustn't let him win you over!

JANE. I'll put these things in the airing cupboard.

SHEILA. He's only doing it to get at David. He's broken up our marriage. Don't let him break up yours as well.

Exit JANE *left.*

Jane . . .

Exit SHEILA *left.*

Enter COLIN *right.*

COLIN. And then one morning you wake up, and it's November, and it's still dark at eight o'clock, and there's nothing in the room but a broken wooden chair, and a few old clothes, and a shelf of unread books, and there's nothing to get up for but the same old struggles and the same old quarrels, and you think, why bother? Who cares what they do to a few grey and grimy houses? What does it matter what happens to a few grey and grubby people? If he wants to build a monument to himself, why shouldn't he? If he can pursue the meaningless without sickening or wearying, why shouldn't the meaningless be his reward?

Enter JANE *right.*

JANE. I've brought your winter overcoat. I'm not staying. I'm not talking. Scarves and pullovers and things in here . . . You look terrible. Are you all right?

COLIN. Fine.

JANE. You're not ill, are you?

COLIN. No.

JANE. What's the matter, then?

COLIN. Loss of appetite. How's David? Is he still enjoying his food?

JANE. I'm not talking about David.

COLIN. I know what he thinks. He thinks he's life and I'm death. But I'm not the one who's sealing the earth with concrete. I'm not the one who's putting up gigantic monumental tombstones.

JANE. It's freezing here. Haven't you got a heater?

COLIN. Or maybe I am death. But how meaningless life would be, if death weren't there to stop it.

JANE. You might feel better if you had a bit more light in here.

COLIN. He's the light, and I'm the dark.

JANE. I suppose I should say thank you for my job. I've only just found out.

COLIN. You and I, Jane. We're both the dark. But then you look up on a clear night and you'll see there's only a dusting of light in all creation. It's a dark universe!

JANE. I'll bring the children on Saturday.

Exit JANE *right.*

Enter DAVID *centre.*

DAVID. Holes. Black holes. Every time I talk to the structural engineers the foundations get bigger! The whole scheme's getting sucked down into these two yawning black holes!

Enter SHEILA *left.*

SHEILA. Or do you just want to be left in peace?

DAVID. Jane not back?

SHEILA. She said she'd be late.

DAVID. Why do I go on with this rotten scheme? I know what it'll be like. The concrete will spall and the ceilings will crack. There'll be condensation under the balconies and leaks in the roof. And the people who live in it will do nothing but complain. They'll hate it. They'll hate me for building it.

SHEILA. You'll feel differently tomorrow. You know how one's feelings change.

DAVID. Yes. I suppose that's why I go on with the scheme. Because if I can get these two towers up that will be something fixed. Two pieces of space will have an outline. As long as those two buildings stand they'll stand in the same place, they'll stand in the same relationship to each other. They won't melt into different shapes. They won't move round each other in the night, or lean against each other for support, or turn their backs on each other, or knock each other down.

SHEILA. It's all my fault, isn't it?

DAVID. They won't feel sorry for each other.

SHEILA. It would be better if I'd never met you.

DAVID. They won't even feel sorry for themselves.

SHEILA. Better if I'd never been born.

DAVID. Anyway, I don't have any choice. I can't just give it up. That's my livelihood. That's my life.

SHEILA. She'd never do anything to hurt you, David. I'm sure of that. She'd never do anything disloyal. You know she wouldn't. Her feelings haven't changed.

DAVID. I wonder if he ever has any doubts.

SHEILA. I couldn't bear it if anything happened to you two. I love you both. *Both*! And that's *my* life. And if anything ever came between you I can't *think* what I'd do! I daren't *think* what I'd do!

JANE (*off*). Me . . .

Exit SHEILA *left.*

Enter JANE *centre.*

I thought I heard Sheila?

DAVID. Went upstairs.

JANE. What?

DAVID. Would you stop it if you could? The scheme. If you could press a button to stop it, and I'd never know, would you press it?

JANE. David . . . All I've said is that I think you're going to have a struggle.

DAVID. I am having a struggle. Would you stop it, Jane?

JANE. I think public opinion has changed since that block collapsed in the East End.

DAVID. That was system-built. These are steel-frame buildings. Would you stop it?

JANE. I think public opinion has changed. That's all I'm saying!

DAVID. I suppose you don't need to say more. You *are* public opinion. Sheila, are you coming in or aren't you?

Enter SHEILA *left.*

SHEILA. I'm sorry.

JANE. I'll go and say hello to the children. I think it's a brilliant scheme, David. Brilliant. Brilliant!

SHEILA. I'm sorry, Jane. I'm so sorry.

JANE *and* SHEILA *go off left.*

DAVID. And then it was spring again. Up came the bright forgotten green. Back came our spirits. A General Election was called, and I was working late and early to finish the scheme design before there were any policy changes at the Ministry. And suddenly there was Colin, sprouting up everywhere like the weeds in the garden. He was in the papers. He was on television. A hero of the Resistance.

Enter SHEILA *centre.*

SHEILA. He's standing now! In the election!

Exit COLIN *right.*

'The most colourful candidate here, though, is undoubtedly Colin Molyneux (Independent). A familiar figure to television viewers in his jeans and tee-shirt with the legend *Get 'em down!* emblazoned across the chest . . . '

DAVID. Wonderful!

SHEILA. ' . . . Molyneux is a former classical scholar who gave up a successful career in journalism . . . '

DAVID. 'Successful career in journalism.' Perfect! Progressive collapse! Get on to 'progressive collapse'.

SHEILA. 'The slogan refers to the notorious twin skyscrapers planned by the local Housing Department . . . '

DAVID. Progressive collapse! Progressive collapse!

SHEILA. 'Molyneux warns that a progressive collapse fifty floors up could bring concrete débris raining down over several acres . . . '

DAVID. 'Several acres.' Good. It's growing. Go on.

SHEILA. 'Molyneux delights his street-corner audiences with gibes at what he calls "North London cultural imperialism" . . . '

DAVID. More! More!

SHEILA. 'There are cheers when he talks about "rarefied Hampstead architects . . . " '

DAVID. Hampstead? I'm going up in the world!

SHEILA. ' " . . . of foreign extraction . . . " '

DAVID. He didn't say that! He can't have said that!

SHEILA. ' " . . . who see districts like this as nothing but vacant lots where they can erect monuments to themselves, as giant boneyards for their own monstrous tombstones." '

DAVID. Tombstones? Tombstones . . . He hates me, doesn't he? He actually hates me.

JANE (*off*). Sorry! Have you eaten . . . ?

Enter JANE *centre.*

Sheila . . . You must be starving . . . Well, first time for everything. I sacked a man today. Terrible! Terrible . . . ! What's the matter?

SHEILA. Colin. He's standing for Parliament now!

JANE. I shouldn't worry. He won't get there.

DAVID. You knew, did you?

JANE. Knew? What, that he was standing? Yes. Didn't you?

DAVID. No. You didn't tell me.

JANE. David, not now. Not this evening. I've had a long day. I'm going to have a long evening.

SHEILA. Well, I ought to be getting back.

JANE. You just came running across to tell him the good news, did you?

SHEILA. I just happened to see it.

DAVID. Don't blame *her*!

JANE. It's funny, though, isn't it? Every time I come in, she goes running out.

DAVID. Don't start on *her*!

JANE. And every time she runs out she leaves a row behind.

SHEILA. Anyway . . .

JANE. Well, now you've started it you might as well stay and enjoy it.

SHEILA. Jane, please; I can't bear this.

DAVID. Go on, Sheila, go home.

JANE. No! She can stay!

DAVID. Sheila . . .

JANE. I said she can stay! So, all right, I didn't tell you Colin was standing. I'm sorry. It didn't seem of any great moment. He won't get in. He'll get sixty-five votes. I'm sorry, though. All right? I've apologised. What else? Is that all? May I sit down now and eat my supper? I've got work to do afterwards.

DAVID. Where's he getting the money from?

JANE. What money?

DAVID. For the Election. Posters, halls, deposit. He's living on social security.

JANE. How should I know?

DAVID. He's not getting it from you? You're not giving him money? It's not our money?

JANE. Is that what you're worrying about?

DAVID. *Is* it our money?

JANE. No!

DAVID. Is he getting it from the people you work for?

JANE. He's getting a little from the Trust.

DAVID. So you do know, then?

JANE. It's not *my* idea! In fact I've consistently opposed it!

DAVID. You said you didn't know. But you do know. Why did you say you didn't know?

JANE. David, I'm not going to be cross-examined like this.

SHEILA. Please!

DAVID. That's the first time you've ever lied to me.

SHEILA. Please! Please!

JANE. Listen, David. Not once, not once have I ever done or said anything that could possibly be disloyal! Not once! I mean, it's ridiculous! I hate the man! I've always hated him! That's all I ever concealed from you!

DAVID. You hate the scheme, too.

JANE. All right, I'll tell you what I think about the scheme. I've never said it to anyone, and I'll never say it again. But if you want to know, I'll tell you. I think those towers of yours are two giant tombstones.

DAVID. Tombstones?

JANE. One for each of us. Anyway, now I've said it.

DAVID. Now you've said it.

JANE. So now you're happy. And don't start snivelling now, Sheila! The row's over!

Exit SHEILA *centre.*

DAVID. Tombstones. It was a coincidence, of course. She'd never heard him use the phrase. She was certain of that. All the same, she wouldn't go and see him again.

Enter COLIN *right.*

The phone rings.

JANE (*into phone*). Hello?

COLIN. Where were you? I've been waiting in all morning.

DAVID. She wouldn't take the children over on Saturday.

COLIN. Can't you hear me, Jane? I said, Where were you?

JANE. I'm sorry, I couldn't come.

DAVID. She should have gone and told him. She shouldn't have waited for him to go out to a phone-box and ring her.

COLIN. Why − is David making difficulties?

JANE. I just couldn't.

COLIN. He's there now, is he?

DAVID. There was no reason not to go and tell him. I certainly wasn't stopping her.

COLIN. I said, He's there now, is he?

JANE. I heard you.

COLIN. I see. Well, tell him we had a torchlight procession last night. Tell him there were five thousand people marching down Basuto Road. From all over London, Jane. All singing. It was like the end of the war. *I* was singing, Jane. You wouldn't have recognised me.

JANE. I'm sorry about the children. I can't bring them any more. You'll have to make some arrangement with Sheila.

Exit JANE *left.*

DAVID. I thought of going to see him myself. I don't know what I was going to say.

Exit COLIN *right.*

I suppose I thought I'd be very generous and understanding. Tell him they were both perfectly free to do everything they could to stop the scheme. We didn't all have to hate each other. I certainly didn't hate him. Something along those lines. Made some contact. It would have been a ridiculous scene. Perhaps I should have gone, though. If I'd gone to him he wouldn't have come to us.

Enter COLIN.

Things might have turned out quite differently. South London might have had another skyline altogether.

Enter JANE *centre.*

JANE. What are you doing here?

DAVID. He wants to see Matt and Lizzie.

JANE. Where are they?

DAVID. Upstairs.

JANE. Where's Sheila?

DAVID. She's upstairs. They're all upstairs. Sheila's in rather a state.

JANE. You shouldn't have come here, Colin.

DAVID. What else could he do?

JANE. Stupid inviting him in.

DAVID. I didn't invite him in! He walked in! He was here when I got back!

JANE. We'll have to start locking that door. You can't just walk in here now, Colin. Things have changed. All it can do is to make trouble. Get him out of here, will you, David? I'm going to see Sheila.

DAVID. Jane, I can't put him out! He's not a cat!

JANE. Well, I don't want him here! I don't want him in my house!

Exit JANE *left.*

DAVID. Colin, I'm sorry. She's right, though. Things *have* changed. We can't all sit round the table together now . . . Colin, look, I don't know how to say this. I know you resent me. I know things haven't always gone well for you in the last few years. I know I've had a certain amount of luck in life . . . Colin, what can I do? I can't apologise for being lucky! And I worked for that luck, and all right, I like my work, but that's not even true — most of my work I don't like! I don't like it anymore than you ever liked yours, because most of it isn't work, it's fighting, and I'm not a fighter! You know that. You're a fighter — I'm not a fighter. I hate fighting . . . Colin, I'm trying to make peace.

Enter JANE *left.*

JANE. I told you to get him out of here.

DAVID. Jane, listen . . .

JANE. Do *I* have to do it?

DAVID. Jane, he won't go until he's arranged something about the children.

JANE. Well, Sheila won't come down until he's gone.

DAVID. And he won't go until he's seen Sheila.

JANE. David, I don't understand. Why are you taking his side?

DAVID. Why am *I* taking his side? *I'm* not taking his side! *I'm* not the one who paid him money to wreck my work! *I'm* not the one who kept creeping off for little chats, and then came back and announced I was turning London into a graveyard!

JANE. David, once and for all, I did *not* give him money! I did *not* discuss your work with him! Ask him, if you don't believe me! He's your friend! Ask him! Ask him!

DAVID. *Me* taking his side! My God!

JANE. Ask him! Ask him! Ask him!

Enter SHEILA *left.*

SHEILA. Shut up! Both of you! Shut up! The children are crying . . . You see what you've done . . . ? Fight *him*! He's the one! He's the destroyer! Look at him, sitting there grinning with pleasure at his handiwork! That's all he can do! Smash and jeer!

JANE. Sheila, go back upstairs.

SHEILA. It's not laughter. You don't know how to laugh. You don't know what laughter's for.

JANE. Sheila, get out of here! Out! Out! Out!

DAVID. Don't start on her now!

JANE. Don't start on her? She's the cause of it all!

DAVID. Sheila? *Sheila's* the cause of it all?

COLIN. She's in love with you.

SHEILA *picks up a steaming stewpan.*

DAVID. Sheila!

JANE. Hot!

DAVID. Don't!

COLIN. Agh!

JANE. Water! Cold water!

DAVID. Here! Towel!

JANE. Phone! Quick!

DAVID. Car! Car! Get him into the car!

JANE. I'll take him. You see to her.

JANE, COLIN *and* DAVID *go off centre.*

SHEILA (*drops pan*). Oh . . .

Enter DAVID *centre.*

I'm sorry, David.

DAVID. In his face, Sheila. In his face!

SHEILA. I wasn't talking about that.

DAVID. No . . . I suppose Jane knew all along.

SHEILA. I'm sorry.

DAVID. Not very clever, am I? Though I don't know quite what I could have done.

SHEILA. You've been so kind to me.

DAVID. Not much use to anyone.

SHEILA. I'll get the children.

DAVID. You don't have to go. This doesn't change anything, does it? You'll go on working. I'll go on working . . .

SHEILA. Always so kind.

DAVID. Now you've burnt your hands.

SHEILA. I'm sorry.

DAVID. I suppose I should find something to put on them . . . In his face, though. I don't know how you could have done that. I don't know anything about anyone.

SHEILA. I'll go and see to the children.

Exit SHEILA *left.*

Enter COLIN *right.*

COLIN. It was worth a few votes, anyway. A mask of surgical dressing, and stories in all the papers — 'Ban-the-towers Colin in mystery attack'. And when polling day came, the outraged electorate rose as one man. Or to be precise, as 173 men. 'Colin Molyneux, Independent, 173 votes'. 173! I wonder what I should have got without the bandages? Poor David, though. My face was painful enough for him. My lost deposit must have been almost more than he could bear.

Enter SHEILA *left.*

DAVID. Don't worry about Colin. He's all right — I saw him again today . . . And don't worry about the children — they know people have fights . . . Don't worry about Jane and me. We're fine. We're going away for a few days together. It doesn't matter if the scheme's a bit late. We know where we stand now . . . 173 votes! Poor Colin. I'll go over and see him again tomorrow — I'll take the children over . . . Don't worry, Sheila!

Exit DAVID *centre.*

COLIN. He'd stand there on the doorstep with my two children held out in front of him like a couple of placatory bottles of wine. He smiled a lot of concerned smiles. Reminded me of some occasion he'd found very affecting when I'd worn a flower in my buttonhole but apparently forgotten my shoes and socks. He was like a dog wanting to be taken in and loved. He gave up in the end, though.

Doorbell. Exit SHEILA *centre.*

Sick visiting, child ferrying — it all stopped the day the scheme stopped.

Enter JANE *and* SHEILA *centre.*

SHEILA. *Stopped?*

JANE. They rang him this morning. Didn't he tell you?

SHEILA. I knew it! I knew it! This was the Housing Committee last night?

JANE. Apparently the Ministry had rejected the revised estimates. I thought you'd know all about it.

SHEILA. David was sure the council would fight them!

JANE. Apparently not.

SHEILA. Oh, Jane, it's all my fault! I held him up! If he'd got the plans finished a month earlier . . . A week earlier, even . . . !

Enter DAVID *centre, with keys.*

Oh, David! It was me, wasn't it? It was me!

DAVID. No, no. It's all in here. ' "We Did It!" says Giantkiller Colin.'

SHEILA. Colin? Colin did it?

DAVID. ' "I always knew we'd wear them down in the end," grinned lone campaigner Colin Molyneux today.'

SHEILA. Colin?

JANE. I thought it was the electricity people? I thought they said it was going to cost another half-million pounds to divert the cable?

DAVID. Yes, or else it was the Ministry, because they wouldn't pay the Generating Board. Or the council, because they wouldn't fight the Ministry. Or that block in the East End. No, it was Colin. Among others. Why wouldn't the Ministry pay? Why couldn't the council fight them? Because no one believes in going high anymore. Because public opinion has changed.

SHEILA. Not *my* opinion, David.

DAVID. No, not your opinion.

JANE. I'm going to put dinner on the table. I've got to work afterwards.

SHEILA. I shall always blame myself.

DAVID. I was too late, that's all. A week, a year — who knows?

SHEILA. It was me.

DAVID. It was people. That's what wrecks all our plans — people.

SHEILA. I can't imagine how you must feel, David.

DAVID. How *I* must feel? I don't know. Like dinner, mostly . . .

COLIN. And that was the end of the Basuto Wars. Basutoland was saved! They didn't pull it down. They did it up.

JANE. We rehabilitated the whole area.

COLIN. The very first improvement they made was to evict me.

SHEILA. I suppose that's when everything changed.

JANE. I suppose that's when we ceased to believe in change.

SHEILA. It was a terrible time. I don't know what David would have done if Jane hadn't had a career. He *knew* he was right about the towers. He wouldn't let go. The practice just went to pieces.

DAVID. Jane, can I slide your stuff back and put dinner on the table?

JANE. Just a minute.

COLIN. We all depended on Jane. At least, I assume it was her influence that got me my job. I assume it was Jane who rehabilitated me.

SHEILA. He got one tower built eventually. It took him seven years. It's only half the height he wanted, and it's not local authority housing, it's private offices. But it's a beautiful building — it won a prize. That didn't help him, though, because it was the recession by then, and there was no work to be had.

DAVID. I've changed my ideas in life. More than once. I never wanted to build high. But you had to then! I never wanted to come down to earth again. But I had to. I'm not ashamed of that. We all have to change, we all have to give. Someone has to, anyway. Nothing would happen in the world otherwise.

COLIN. Rehabilitation schemes. That's what I write about. That's what I live in — a rehab. A new word. A new world of tastefully uniform front doors and tastefully paved pedestrian precincts. I sometimes feel I'd like to demolish the lot, and put up a few skyscrapers. So I suppose *I* haven't changed.

DAVID. We all change. Everything changes. I'm rather proud of some of those rehab schemes I've done for Jane. I'm happy enough, anyway. We're happy enough . . . Look, I can't keep the meal hot indefinitely.

JANE. Just coming.

SHEILA. I see David's building sometimes when I'm on my way to my sessions with Dr Medtner. It makes me think of . . . I don't know — summer coming, the feeling that things are going to change.

DAVID. The only one who never changed was Sheila. She went on believing to the end, like some old Stalinist. Still does, for all I know. She moved away when they divorced. I couldn't keep her on, of course — I couldn't keep anyone on. It was best for her, anyway — she'd got completely dependent on us. It was pulling her down — it was part of her depression. I think Jane found her a job somewhere.

COLIN. Even Sheila's being rehabilitated. Or so I gather from Lizzie. She goes to see some woman of Central European extraction in Hampstead.

SHEILA. Dr Medtner says I can learn to change. I have the

capacity for happiness, she says.

COLIN. Apparently this woman's got a husband who's a doctor, too. An eye-specialist, according to Lizzie. 'Lizzie,' I said, 'have the white stick ready.'

DAVID. Shall I put something over it to stop it drying up? What do you think?

JANE. I suppose I've changed. I've learnt one thing from working with people, anyway: they want to be told what to do.

DAVID. Or do you want to eat as you work?

JANE. That's what I long for. I know that. Just to be told what to do . . . Dinner? Well, slide this stuff back and put it on the table, then.

DAVID. I drove down Basuto Road the other day. The sun was shining, and some woman was standing in a doorway with her children and laughing, and it all looked quite bright and cheerful.

SHEILA. Basuto Road. Yes, and at once it's summer, and everything is about to change.

COLIN. I did one good thing in this world, anyway. I helped poor old David. I saved him from a lifetime of public execration.

JANE. Basuto Road? It's strange; the cloud moves on, and there's the landscape out in sunshine again.

DAVID. Basuto Road. There's the whole history of human ideas in that one name.

JANE. And yes! I was! I was happy!

DAVID. Laughing and laughing. But what she was laughing about I never discovered.

Curtain.

The Master Playwrights

Collections of plays by the best-known modern playwrights in value-for money paperbacks.

John Arden	PLAYS: ONE *Serjeant Musgrave's Dance, The Workhouse Donkey, Armstrong's Last Goodnight*
Brendan Behan	THE COMPLETE PLAYS *The Hostage, The Quare Fellow, Richard's Cork Leg, Moving Out, A Garden Party, The Big House*
Edward Bond	PLAYS: ONE *Saved, Early Morning, The Pope's Wedding* PLAYS: TWO *Lear, The Sea, Narrow Road to the Deep North, Black Mass, Passion*
Noël Coward	PLAYS: ONE *Hay Fever, The Vortex, Fallen Angels, Easy Virtue* PLAYS: TWO *Private Lives, Bitter Sweet, The Marquise, Post-Mortem* PLAYS: THREE *Design for Living, Cavalcade, Conversation Piece*, and *Hands Across the Sea, Still Life* and *Fumed Oak* from *Tonight at 8.30* PLAYS: FOUR *Blithe Spirit, This Happy Breed, Present Laughter*, and *Ways and Means, The Astonished Heart* and *Red Peppers* from *Tonight at 8.30* PLAYS: FIVE *Relative Values, Look After Lulu, Waiting in the Wings, Suite in Three Keys*
Henrik Ibsen	*Translated and introduced by Michael Meyer* PLAYS: ONE *Ghosts, The Wild Duck, The Master Builder* PLAYS: TWO *A Doll's House, An Enemy of the People, Hedda Gabler* PLAYS: THREE *Rosmersholm, Little Eyolf, The Lady from the Sea* PLAYS: FOUR *John Gabriel Borkman, The Pillars of Society, When We Dead Awaken*